November Ever After

November Ever After

*A memoir of tragedy and triumph
in the wake of the
1970 Marshall football plane crash*

Craig T. Greenlee

iUniverse, Inc.
Bloomington

November Ever After
A memoir of tragedy and triumph in the wake of the 1970 Marshall
football plane crash

iUniverse books may be ordered through booksellers or by contacting:

iUniverse
1663 Liberty Drive
Bloomington, IN 47403
www.iuniverse.com
1-800-Authors (1-800-288-4677)

ISBN: 978-1-4620-0404-1 (sc)
ISBN: 978-1-4620-0403-4 (ebk)

Printed in the United States of America

iUniverse rev. date: 07/22/11

Contents

Acknowledgments...xi

Introduction..xiii

Chapter One   Back in the Day..1

Chapter Two   Season of Challenges......................................14

Chapter Three   Chilly Racial Climate.....................................24

Chapter Four   Unforgettable, Unbelievable 35

Chapter Five   Homegoing Caravan 57

Chapter Six   They Were Spared...69

Chapter Seven   Moving On...82

Chapter Eight   Etched in Memory.......................................103

Chapter Nine   Media Treatment of the Tragedy 124

Chapter Ten   It's Always with You....................................138

Appendix 147

To my mother, Winnie F. Greenlee, the most determined person I have ever known. Your desire and ability to succeed in spite of long odds is an inspiration to people of all ages.

Honoring Those Who Perished

November 14, 1970

Coaches
Al Carelli, Jr., Jim "Shorty" Moss, Rick Tolley,
Deke Brackett, Frank Loria

Players
Jim Adams, Mark Andrews, Michael Blake, Dennis Blevins, Willie Bluford,
Larry Brown, Thomas Brown, Roger Childers, Stuart Cottrell,
Rick Dardinger, David DeBord, Kevin Gilmore, David Griffith, Art Harris,
Bob Harris, Bobby Hill, Joe Hood, Tom Howard, Marcello Lajterman,
Rick Lech, Barry Nash, Pat Norrell, Bob Patterson, Scottie Reese,
Jack Repasy, Larry Sanders,
Al Saylor, Art Shannon, Ted Shoebridge, Allen Skeens, Jerry Stainback,
Robert VanHorn,
Roger Vanover, Freddy Wilson, John Young, Tom Zborill

Other Staff
Charles Kautz, Gene Morehouse, Jim Schroer, Donald Tackett,
Gary George

Fans
Charles Arnold, Rachel Arnold, Donald Booth, Dr. Joseph Chambers,
Peggy Chambers, Shirley Ann Hagley, Dr. Ray Hagley,
Arthur Harris Sr., Emmett Heath, Elaine Heath, Cynthia Jarrell,
James Jarrell, Kenneth Jones, Jeff Nathan, Brian O'Connor,
Michael Prestera, Dr. Glenn Preston, Phyllis Preston, Courtney Proctor,
Dr. Herbert Proctor, Helen Ralsten, Murrill Ralsten, Parker Ward,
Norman Weichmann

Flight Crew
Captain Frank Abbott, Jerry Smith, Charlene Poat, Patricia Vaught,
Danny Deese

Acknowledgments

The completion of this work is not a case of happenstance, nor is it a solo undertaking. For those reasons, it's fitting and proper that I recognize those who have contributed immeasurably to this endeavor.

First and foremost, to my Lord and Savior Jesus Christ who is the same today, yesterday, and forevermore. I remain ever thankful to the Lamb of God who is forever faithful.

My wife Cynthia: Luv ya, "Sweets." You are my gift from above. Can't say enough about how much I value you as my confidant and life partner.

Dr. Ed Carter: Keep on pressing on to the mark of the high calling in Jesus Christ. Blessings always for you and Death Unto Life Ministries, which continues to transform lives by the power of the Holy Spirit.

Dickie Carter: Immense thanks for being so willing to share your perspective. Your story has been ignored for far too long. And I'm glad that you allowed me to help you convey your innermost thoughts and feelings about your football-playing days at Marshall University.

Felix Jordan: There's no way I could have done this without some input from you. We didn't get a chance to talk in great detail. But during that time, as I listened to you, I came away with an even clearer understanding of those events from over forty years ago that will always be etched in our memories.

Macie Lugo, Janice Cooley, and Debbie (Bailey) Bowen: I can only imagine the inner turmoil that you've gone through. And I realize that it wasn't easy for you to recount some still very painful memories. You spoke from the depths of your hearts, and for that you have my everlasting thanks.

To the remainder of the Marshall University family: Thank you for allowing me to thoroughly test your long-term memories. Your descriptive recollections were invaluable.

Pastor Gregory Dennis: The example you set as a Bible-believing, Bible-preaching, Bible-teaching instrument of God encourages and blesses me over and over again.

Terry Oberle: Whether you realize it or not, you did me a huge favor by not publishing my story as a lengthy newspaper feature. Had it run, I probably wouldn't have given much thought to writing this book.

Ralph Turner: You had not yet attained professor status in those days when I was one of your journalism students at MU. But as far as I was concerned, you were already a Ph.D-caliber mentor. Your calm and reassuring demeanor did wonders for my confidence level as a fledgling writer.

Ernie Salvatore: You gave me my first media job while I was still a college undergraduate (*Herald-Dispatch* sports department). The pay was nothing to write home about (the minimum wage of $1.60 per hour), but the experience made it all worthwhile. Working under your tutelage helped me to get a good feel for what I could accomplish in a "real-world" setting.

John Toner: I deeply appreciate you providing a nurturing environment and the tools to help me expand my horizons as a military journalist.

Horace and Deltra Bonner: Quite a few years have passed since you first suggested that I consider writing a book. Apparently, you noticed something that I clearly overlooked. Thanks for the vote of confidence.

The staff at iUniverse: As a first-time book author, your patience and professionalism are all that I could ever hope for. Throughout the publishing process, I've learned so much about the nuances of communicating through the written word. So now, I view the craft of writing in an entirely different light.

Introduction

Joan C. Edwards Stadium, home of Marshall University football, stands in stark contrast to the Thundering Herd's old stomping grounds from over four decades ago: Fairfield Stadium. The 38,000-seat facility known as "The Joan" sits on the eastern edge of campus and has all the requisite amenities found in modern-day athletic arenas: a plush playing surface, luxury suites with closed-circuit television, 4,300-plus chair-backed seats, plus a state-of-the-art scoreboard with video and statistics display capabilities. The stadium's design allows for expansion to a capacity of 55,000.

The location of the old stadium wasn't nearly as convenient. A twenty-minute drive across town from campus would get you to old Fairfield Stadium (depending on game-day traffic). Back then, Marshall and two city high schools played their home games there. In the late '60s, old Fairfield, which held around 12,000 fans, had more than its share of divots. In the days before artificial turf was installed, Fairfield's playing surface looked more like a badly kept fairway. There's no telling how many long touchdown runs never happened because of the potholes that caused breakaway runners to stumble and fall before reaching the end zone.

Back then, football was not the kingpin that it is now. At that time, Marshall was still searching for a formula that would help build a winning tradition. For a brief moment in time, Thundering Herd football had the makings of something that would have been great for years to come. But a recruiting scandal followed by a tragic plane crash put a huge dent in those plans. It didn't seem possible that the school would overcome such serious setbacks.

There's nobody else around who can tell this story from the perspective of a former player who experienced the promise, agony, and uplift associated with Marshall University football in the late '60s/early '70s. The year of '68 is important to note. About one-third of the players who died in the crash first came to Marshall in '68, and they were the nucleus of the '70 team.

I'm the only living link with a connection to the Herd's undefeated freshman team of '68, who played in '69 and/or '70, and who also took part in the efforts to keep football on the school's athletic menu. Spring practice of '71 was a critical juncture for a shattered program confronted with the huge task of reviving itself. I played safety at Marshall for two seasons and left the team after my sophomore year because I lost the desire to play. Had I chosen to stay, I probably wouldn't be alive today. I could've been a passenger on that plane.

The tragedy did spark a brief comeback for me as a player. After the crash, I came out for spring ball and reclaimed my spot on the roster. But once preseason drills started in August, I could no longer ignore the reality that I didn't want to play football any longer. A few weeks before the '71 season opener, I quit the team and never returned.

In the years following the crash, there have been some big-name athletes who wore the green and white. But there was a time when Marshall had it all going with a growing arsenal of talented players who could have put the school on the football map much sooner. Eventually, Marshall got its reward in the 1990s—a time in which the Herd won 114 games to validate itself as the winningest program in college football for that decade.

I have some in-depth knowledge of what life was like when Marshall lost most of its football team in a fiery plane crash. I was there. I knew most of the victims. But this book isn't strictly about my point of view. Former schoolmates are heavy contributors to this work. Collectively, we share our memories of the hope, horror, and ultimate victory as people who witnessed Marshall football survive tough times and eventually rise to prominence many years later.

November 14, 1970. The team was returning home after playing a Saturday afternoon game at East Carolina University. The chartered flight was only minutes away from reaching the runway. Before the plane could land, it hit some treetops and crashed on a hillside, killing everybody onboard. In the days leading up to the crash, there was apprehension among some of the players. They had an uneasy feeling about leaving town for the road trip on Friday the 13th. Some were supposed to make the trip but for different reasons did not go.

John Hagan, the football team's equipment manager, was uncomfortable about flying. That's why he decided to use a truck to transport the Herd's football equipment to East Carolina and back. One of the most eerie reminders of the tragedy is a photograph that was taken just six days after the crash. In that picture, Hagan stands among a giant heap of helmets, shoulder pads, and other football equipment in Marshall's locker room.

Because I was so close to the situation as a student and former player, I made a conscious decision to avoid reading every news account about the tragedy in the days following November 14. As a journalism major, I was supposed to have an insatiable hunger to learn everything I could about this catastrophe. That was not the case for me. I arrived at my decision on the morning after the crash when I picked up the local Sunday newspaper. In looking over the headlines, it was evident that the coverage was extensive and thorough. But there was only so much I really wanted to know.

The horror and trauma of it all left me feeling like I was carrying a fifty-pound weight around my neck. It was more than I wanted to deal with, both emotionally and psychologically. I was satisfied with selectively choosing what I wanted to know. All that changed when I started to do background research for this book, thirty-something years after the fact.

In order to paint a fair and accurate picture of what happened that night and the days that followed, I realized that, for the sake of credibility, I needed to become more familiar with the particulars. And anyway, this is not about honing in on gory details. I've heard my share of horror stories about what the rescue workers saw that night.

November Ever After examines the impact the crash had on a school, its football program, and those who were left behind. There's a racial issue associated with this story that's rarely mentioned. The day before the tragedy—Friday the 13th—a massive brawl involving blacks and whites broke out after an intramural football game. Racial tensions reached a fever pitch that day, raising the likelihood that an ugly race riot might occur. The following night, all apprehension evaporated because of the crash, which touched blacks and whites equally and deeply. The tragic deaths of the football players set a tone for racial reconciliation. The brawl became a quickly fading memory. People forgot all about black-white confrontations. Instead, the focus was all about attending the funerals of our fallen schoolmates. That's all that really mattered.

Ironically, it was one of Marshall's black football players who helped keep the peace. Larry Brown managed to coax an angry crowd of blacks and whites to calm down in the aftermath of a bruising black-white fight.

His efforts prevented an escalation of hostilities that could have led to a dangerous altercation. By eight o'clock the next night, Brown was dead.

It's been over forty years since these events happened. So the question that begs to be answered is this: why write this book now? Bottom-line answer: It's time—time to shed some much-needed light on aspects of the Marshall saga that haven't been previously covered in any book, documentary, or movie that I'm aware of.

Until I was compelled to pursue this project, there was never a time that I felt the need to have my curiosity satisfied about exactly what happened on that traumatic night. Six days after the crash, I took a flight out of that same airport to attend the funeral of my best friend who was one of the seventy-five victims. I never looked for any visual signs of the disaster. Clean-up of the crash scene had not been completed.

On take-off from Tri-State Airport and again on the return trip, I made a conscious effort *to not look* out the passenger window. I simply didn't want to visualize what it must have been like for the people on that plane in the moments before their demise.

Agony is part of Marshall's football history, but there's another facet that has always made this story an intriguing one. Even though there were some endless days of despair, there were enough spirit-lifting days to balance the scales. Through all the turmoil, a decimated football program was able to get itself off life support and back in the saddle to compete and eventually establish a winning mind-set. It didn't happen right away. It would take another fourteen years *after* the crash before Marshall would have a winning season.

Once the Herd got over that hump, the program began to soar to new levels. Aside from winning two national championships, the Thundering Herd has a 6-2 record in bowl games since upgrading to the NCAA Football Bowl Subdivision (formerly known as Division I-A) in '97. That's a remarkable reversal for a program that found itself in dire straits over four decades ago.

While the football program hasn't been able to match the excellence of the 1990s, it has reached a level of respectability that greatly exceeds its lowly status in the late '60s and all of the '70s. In those days, there was no such thing as taking victory for granted.

Forty-something years is a long time for memories to linger and not be recorded. Should it take that much time to finalize conclusions about events that took place so long ago? I call it not-so-ancient history. All this happened during the formative years of being a young adult. This was before marriage, before parenthood, and long before any grandchildren.

Now I'm pushing past sixty on the age-o-meter, but I'm far from ready to enter geezerhood. The world is so much different now from what it was back then. In my freshman year, tuition at Marshall University was a mere $129 for an in-state student ($429 out-of-state). It was actually cheaper for me to go to school in West Virginia as an out-of-state student than it was for me to go to school back home in Jacksonville, Florida, as an in-state student.

At that time, Marshall's student body numbered around 8,200, and a good portion of those were commuters. Fast-forward forty-plus years: Marshall's student population has increased by 68 percent. In the meantime, the school has established nationally respected programs in medicine and nursing, forensic science, law, business, and journalism.

Chapter One

Back in the Day

Hope and a promise lured me to Marshall University in 1968. As a black teenager raised in Jacksonville, Florida, Marshall was a most unlikely choice. Up to that point in my life, the black culture was all that I had ever known. With the exception of a summer job or two, I had no interaction with white people. Marshall, a predominantly white school in Huntington, West Virginia, was the cultural opposite of what I was accustomed to. Keep in mind that in the late '60s, the Deep South was still shamelessly segregated. As things turned out, though, my dream of playing college football would eventually overrule any desire I had to stay in my self-imposed comfort zone.

Back in the day, the vast majority of Jacksonville's black high school graduates attended Florida A&M University or Bethune-Cookman College. I knew by the spring semester of my senior year at William Raines High School that I would make every effort to attend an out-of-state school. I wanted to go somewhere different, somewhere that was hundreds of miles away from home. What I didn't want was to feel like I was in high school all over again. More than anything, I wanted a new experience. I had zero interest in being in a place where many of the other freshmen already knew my name.

By the late '60s, the Vietnam conflict had escalated. College served as a refuge for young guys between eighteen and twenty-six who didn't want to go to the army. Full-time college students were given deferments, which meant that as long as they remained in school they didn't have to worry about being drafted and possibly going overseas to fight a war in

Southeast Asia. Yes, I was "draftable," but I never had any concerns about being drafted. My plans for furthering my education had nothing to do with avoiding the military. In my mind, college was where I was supposed to be.

Johnson C. Smith University, a predominantly black college in Charlotte, North Carolina, was my first and only choice. But right around high school graduation, I started receiving letters and postcards from Marshall, promising me an athletic scholarship if I made the team as a walk-on. All summer long, I kept Marshall in mind, but only as a back-up just in case things fell through with J.C. Smith. I just knew that I was bound for North Carolina.

All that changed by midsummer. J.C. Smith had not sent any enrollment paperwork, so I figured there was no interest. That's when I decided to take my chances on a school that I knew absolutely nothing about. Most people back home thought I was going to Marshall College in Texas, which was really Wiley College, a black school located in Marshall, Texas. When I told them I was going to West Virginia, the jokes started and never ceased. Since separation of the races was still a fact of life, there weren't many blacks attending mainstream schools in the South at that time.

Friends reminded me that I would probably be the only black on the team and that I would be playing ball with hillbillies, a stereotype of West Virginia strongly reinforced by television shows like *The Real McCoy* and *The Beverly Hillbillies*. I was also told that I'd have to dress differently. They envisioned me wearing white tube socks with dress shoes and high-water pants—a definite no-no for a fashion-conscious soul brother like myself.

I was surprised to discover that so many people were geographically challenged as to West Virginia's location. Folks tended to believe that it was a section of Virginia, which at one time was true. But that was before West Virginia became a state in 1863. One of the reasons West Virginia seceded was because its people didn't want to be part of the pro-slavery Confederacy led by Virginia. My friends wanted to know how far Huntington, West Virginia, is from Richmond (Virginia's state capital). All they had to do was look at a map to see that West Virginia and Virginia are separate states just like North Carolina and South Carolina or North Dakota and South Dakota.

It still amazes me that I ended up at Marshall. Was this a matter of coincidence, or was it destiny? The *day before* I was scheduled to leave home for West Virginia, I received a special delivery package from J.C. Smith with all the paperwork that I should have received weeks earlier. I was relieved that they finally sent me a package. On the other hand, I was miffed that it took so long.

Since I had already purchased my plane ticket and informed Marshall's coaches that I'd come in as a walk-on, my sole focus was getting to West Virginia. This was not a casual journey on a jet. I was on a mission. This was a business trip and I dressed the part: wintergreen-colored herringbone sports coat, dress shirt, necktie, dark trousers, and dress shoes, complete with a London Fog hat that matched the color of my sports coat.

On my flight's arrival, the weather was sunny and clear with a few scattered clouds. All I could see from the passenger window were hills and more hills as far as my eyes could see. Geographically, this area was so much different from Florida. Huntington is hilly compared to Jacksonville. But the city's terrain is relatively flat when compared to other West Virginia cities, such as Charleston, Bluefield, and Morgantown.

Nothing was going to stop me from achieving my goal of earning a roster spot on a college team. Motivation was not a problem, and neither was the possibility that I might get homesick. I dreaded the thought of returning home and having to answer an endless number of questions about why I didn't make it. For me, that would have been the ultimate embarrassment. Some way, somehow, I was going to make the most of this opportunity.

Back then, football was definitely a second-class sport at Marshall. However, a dramatic metamorphosis began to take place when Perry Moss took over as head coach in 1968. At that juncture, Marshall was in freefall as a member of the Mid-American Conference. In the two seasons prior to Moss's arrival, the Herd was woeful at two wins and eighteen losses. Things would not change immediately because NCAA rules prohibited freshmen from playing varsity sports. Marshall went 0-9-1 in Moss's first season, but help was on the way.

Moss's first crop of recruits, the freshman class of 1968, had an abundance of size, speed, and athleticism. At six feet, 160 pounds, I was not one of those *ripped* individuals. What I lacked in size, I made up for with good hands and better-than-decent speed (clocked 4.6 seconds in the forty-yard dash). Plus, I had the versatility to contribute as a wide receiver, defensive back, and kick returner. As for my weight room numbers, those were nonexistent because I never lifted weights. Speed and quickness were my fortes, and those tools had always served me well. I made the team as a walk-on wide receiver/defensive back. By the time our season began, I was the starter at free safety.

More than one hundred players showed up for preseason practice in August. It was like an NFL training camp. The athletes, many of whom were black, came mostly from the Southern states. Marshall didn't have many black students when the '68 freshman class arrived. The previous year, the school's head count was in the neighborhood of 7,000, which included an estimated 125 blacks. (Documentation of the number of blacks attending MU in '67 is not available.)

It was never said publicly, but it was clear that Moss's master plan for a football turnaround centered on bringing in large numbers of black athletes. So it was hardly surprising that roughly half of the freshman football team's sixty-player roster was black. Fast-forward by forty-plus years and the number count reveals some interesting findings. In the fall semester of 2010, Marshall had 13,718 students. Of that total, blacks made up 4.6 percent of the student body. In the meantime, there was a noticeable boost in the number of black football players, compared to back in the day. Black athletes comprised 61 percent of the Thundering Herd's ninety-eight-player roster for the 2010 season.

In '68, the coaches needed a way to help them sort through all the new faces. We had to put two-inch wide tape on the front of our helmets and write our names on the tape with a felt-tip marker just so the coaches could tell who was who.

Dickie Carter, a sophomore running back that year, has vivid recollections about that first class of recruits brought in by Moss. He couldn't help but take notice. The varsity occupied one of the practice fields and the freshmen practiced on an adjacent field. Those practice fields, which were mostly dirt with patches of grass here and there, had no need for manicuring. One of the fields was surrounded by a quarter-mile gravel track. There were days when the combination of dirt, gravel, and swirling winds transformed that field into a dust bowl.

"I remember all the different-color jerseys," Dickie told me during an interview. "It seemed like there were enough new players to make two or three teams. And when I looked around and saw so many blacks, it was something that I wasn't used to seeing (at Marshall). After watching the players for a while, I got the feeling that these new guys are gonna be all right."

4

With so many players from so many different places, everyone on that freshman team had his own story to tell about coming to West Virginia to play ball. One of the most frequently repeated stories involved a recruit from Louisiana (I can't remember who). On the long ride from Bayou country to Huntington, West Virginia, the Greyhound bus made its regularly scheduled stop in Bluefield, West Virginia. As soon as the prospect got off the bus to walk around and stretch his legs, he was approached by an inquisitive baggage handler who said, "Hey, son, where ya' headed?"

"Goin' to Marshall," the recruit answered.

As he conducted a visual inspection of the recruit, the baggage handler asked if he played football.

"Sure do."

For some reason, he wasn't convinced that the bulky youngster really was a football player. "Hmmmm. I don't know. I heard they got some beef up there at Marshall. How tall are ya'?"

"Six feet, three."

"How much you weigh?"

"Two hundred and sixty pounds."

After taking another look at the husky specimen, he declared, "Hmmmm. *You might make it!*"

The black players on the freshman team brought some of their culture with them. Most of us had attended all-black high schools in the Deep South. As a result, we were accustomed to having prayer—as a team—prior to leaving the locker room before the start of a game.

Before kickoff in our season opener against the University of Kentucky, the coaches gave their pregame talks. And then somebody asked when we were going to pray. Everybody just looked around at each another, as if they were waiting to see who would speak up. Nobody appeared to be interested in volunteering.

The delay and uncertainty prompted me to start praying, even though I had never prayed aloud in front of a group of people. It's not like I had a background in ministry. All I could think about were the prayers I heard while growing up in the Episcopal Church as a youngster. I also thought about how thankful I was to be in college and to have the opportunity to play football. As things turned out, I became the one who was designated to pray for the team before the start of every game. After that first prayer, all the players called me "Preacher." One of the freshman team coaches nicknamed me "Rabbi."

The influx of new talent produced immediate results and gave hope for a brighter future. Marshall's freshmen went 5-0 and delivered surprising wins over Kentucky and MAC powerhouse Ohio University. By mid-October, the freshmen had developed such a high level of confidence that we more than held our own in those Monday scrimmages against the varsity, which Coach Moss often referred to as the "Toilet Bowl." The players moving up to varsity from the unbeaten freshman team were viewed as the saviors-in-waiting for a program that had fallen on hard times.

Talk about swagger. As freshmen, we knew we could handle the varsity because our talent level was so much higher. As it was, competition among the freshmen was so fierce that if you got hurt, you might not get your starting position back. With the rookies getting so much attention, I figured the varsity guys might have some hard feelings. If that was the case, it was never spoken. And besides, why would anyone be envious? Everybody looked forward to the day when Marshall would no longer serve as a bottom-feeder to be pushed around, intimidated, and bullied by opponents.

"A football field is the only place in America where you can hit somebody and it's legal."

We heard those words often from freshman coach Pete Kondos, nicknamed "Pistol Pete" by the players. And it became obvious, even to the casual observer, that we took those words to heart. Being physical was the freshman team's hallmark, especially on defense, which had eight blacks in the starting lineup.

Toward the end of the season, the Marshall freshmen had developed a following. The team got its share of media coverage, not as much as the varsity but more than what most freshman teams usually get. The varsity didn't win a game that year (0-9-1) and we didn't lose a game. Marshall's frosh drew a decent crowd (around 3,000) for its only home game, which just happened to be the season finale. We won handily over West Virginia Tech in a game that gave the local folks a preview of Marshall's talent level for the next season.

Afterward, we returned to campus. It wasn't long before a dozen black youngsters who were at the game stopped by the dorm for a spur-of-the-moment visit. The coaches let us keep our jerseys from that game, but I didn't keep mine for long. One of the youngsters pleaded for a souvenir, so I gave him my jersey as a keepsake. I felt like somewhat of a celebrity after that. We had finished the year undefeated and everyone familiar with Marshall was ecstatic about its football future.

Marshall's freshman class of '68 had a cast of characters. For me, Robinson Crusoe, Isaac Tatum, and Larry Nelson rank among the most memorable.

Crusoe, a black wide receiver from Mobile, Alabama, was always the topic of conversation. He was named after the main character in the well-known literary classic written by Daniel Defoe. The novel focuses on Crusoe, a castaway who was stranded for twenty-something years on a remote tropical island located near Venezuela. Nobody ever called out Crusoe by his first name. When the weather was warm, Crusoe typically dressed in his beachcomber attire: sleeveless T-shirts, cut-off shorts, and sandals.

Tatum, whose home was Louisiana, didn't have the look of a physically chiseled linebacker. But in his case, looks were deceiving. Tatum, six feet, three inches and 240 pounds, was extremely slew-footed. People who are slew-footed do not walk with their feet pointed straight ahead. Instead, their feet point outward, just like a duck. This looks awkward, but it was never a problem for Tatum. He could cover ground quickly and match strides with most running backs (clocked at 4.6 seconds in the forty-yard dash). With his size and speed, he could have played any linebacker position or done just as well as a defensive end.

Tatum was so unconventional because of his slew-footedness. On the field, he resembled a sprinting penguin roaming from sideline to sideline. Not sure why he never got any playing time. There was never a question about his athletic ability. Tatum left school after that first year and joined the US Navy. I don't know if he made a career of it or not.

Nelson, at five feet, seven inches and 180 pounds, was a stand-out linebacker/running back from Danora, Pennsylvania. During preseason camp, Larry got his nickname while we were watching film of one of our scrimmages. Coach Kondos complimented Nelson on a hit and then told us how Larry's build reminded him of a Butterball turkey. From that time on, Nelson, one of my freshman roomies, was known as "Butterball."

The city of Huntington is located in the southwestern part of West Virginia known to many as the Tri-State. The city borders the states of Ohio and Kentucky, and the Ohio River is just a few minutes' drive from campus. It doesn't take long to cross state lines if you're in downtown Huntington. You can still walk or ride a bike across the downtown bridge and be in Ohio in a matter of minutes. Or you could drive twenty minutes or so in the opposite direction and find yourself in Kentucky.

Huntington is College Town, USA, and that's not likely to ever change. The city's health-care complex and Marshall's School of Medicine have experienced significant growth. The blue-collar workforce still has a presence but not nearly to the extent of the late '60s. Whether you're in a restaurant or a bank, you can't help but notice the visible reminders (banners, calendars, MU sports photos, and other memorabilia) that validate the city's status as home of the beloved Thundering Herd.

Coming to Huntington in the late '60s was culture shock for me. At that time, Huntington's population was around 70,000, a substantial drop-off from my hometown. Nicknamed the "Gateway City," Jacksonville's population was around 514,000, with blacks comprising about 20 percent of the population. Huntington, by contrast, didn't have nearly as many blacks. I estimate 3,000, maybe 4,000. Back home, I was used to visiting black folks who lived in all four corners of the city and every place in between. In Huntington, you could ride through the black community in twenty to twenty-five minutes.

I soon discovered that I'd need to make some drastic adjustments in my radio-listening habits. Since Jacksonville had a lot more black folks, it had a couple of black radio stations that played nothing but soul music. By contrast, Huntington was geared more to rock music and country and western. Back home, I was accustomed to listening to The Temptations, James Brown, and Gladys Knight & The Pips on a regular basis. If I was going to listen to music on the radio in West Virginia, I had to get used to a steady diet of Blood, Sweat & Tears, Bob Dylan, and Steppenwolf. Soul music wasn't exactly null and void. Huntington radio stations played rhythm and blues songs every now and then.

For me and the other black students, the only decent source of soul music was located hundreds of miles away in Nashville, Tennessee. We tuned in to WLAC on the AM dial, and we had a jamming good time whenever we could get a strong signal. Listening to WLAC was like being at home. Tuning in to a radio station in Tennessee, though, was a hit or miss proposition. We could get a good signal on clear nights from around eleven o'clock to the wee hours of the early morning. This was far from ideal, but it was better than nothing at all. And it did give me a break from Engelbert Humperdinck.

My music-listening habits weren't the only cultural adjustment I'd be forced to make. Getting acclimated to different genres of music was one thing. It was quite another to learn how the use of one word can produce vastly different responses among people who grew up in different parts of the United States. When it comes to cultural differences, things aren't always what they appear to be.

Case in point: the use of the word *boy*.

It didn't take long for offensive lineman Ed Carter to find out that a word he perceived to be offensive was not a big deal when spoken by somebody from West Virginia.

For the black athletes who grew up in the South, attending Marshall was our first time being in a multiracial environment. Literally and figuratively speaking, integration was a brand-new ball game for us.

For black males living in the South at that time, being referred to as "boy" was an unwelcome reminder of racism, which had begun to diminish to some extent by the time we became high school seniors. Being called "boy" was not something that any of us expected. Quite frankly, the very mention of that word coming from a Caucasian mouth could immediately incite fisticuffs.

During his freshman year, Ed Carter found himself in such a situation. He was among a group of black and white students who were having a discussion. One of the white students called him "boy," and the mood turned tense in a hurry.

"Until then, I never had any problems with anybody," Ed said. "Where I grew up (in Texas), if somebody called you 'boy,' it was the same as using the *n* word. I didn't take too kindly to that, and a friend of mine had to pull me off the guy. My friend kept telling me that the guy I was upset with didn't mean anything by it. He told me that everybody—blacks and whites—does that in West Virginia. So, then I understood that that's just the way it is."

In the spring of 1969, there was a very noticeable air of excitement about what was in store for Thundering Herd football. Another batch of blue-chippers and quality walk-ons was headed to Marshall for the upcoming fall season. But little did any of us know that the program would find itself in deep trouble in the coming months. Moss would never get the opportunity to coach his first recruiting class at the varsity level.

That summer, the bottom fell out. An investigation revealed that the school committed more than one hundred recruiting violations, which led to indefinite suspension from the Mid-American Conference and being placed on probation by the National Collegiate Athletic Association. Moss was fired as head coach and reassigned to non-coaching duties.

I always thought it was so strange that a coach at a losing program could get busted like that. Usually, schools that break the rules aren't caught for wrongdoing until *after* they've become successful.

My knowledge of the college recruiting process was next to nil. I didn't get much playing time as a back-up quarterback in my senior year of high school. So I was really an unknown commodity. I never had any phone conversations with college coaches. Recruiters never made any visits to the Greenlee household.

I didn't need to be a Rhodes Scholar to help me figure out that a position switch was in order. In those days, playing quarterback at a white school in the South was not an option for the black athlete. My best shot at making the grade at Marshall would be as a pass catcher or pass defender. The fact that I attracted some interest as a back-up quarterback was not all that surprising. It's not like I was some marginal scrub sitting at the end of the bench. As a high school senior, I was the starting quarterback until a knee injury suffered a week before the season opener caused me to miss six games.

Unbeknownst to me at the time, Marshall engaged in a massive letter-writing campaign to high school football coaches all across the South. Coach Perry Moss wanted to bring in as many players as possible, and he didn't care about skin color. Since MU was a perennial loser, Moss searched far and wide for talent that could deliver an immediate turnabout. Marshall sent letters to some of my high school teammates and a few guys I played against. As things turned out, though, I was the only player from Jacksonville to cast my lot with the Thundering Herd that year. I knew it was a risk to travel so far from home to a school I had no familiarity with whatsoever. To me, the risk was worth it.

Marshall's football freshmen of '68 fared so well that fan interest soared to unprecedented levels. Expectations were so high that it was inevitable that at some point somebody, somewhere, would raise enough questions to trigger an investigation. How was it that a perennial loser was able to suddenly attract so many top-grade athletes? If the 1968 freshman class was a sign of things to come, it wouldn't take long for the Herd's transformation from weak link to powerhouse to take full effect.

In 1968, it was common knowledge that certain players got cash payments and special favors. All this came to light when one of the pay-for-play athletes decided to quit going to spring practice. The player was informed that his payments would cease if he didn't return. The player, whose identity has never been revealed publicly, told a relative about his situation. This relative, who had strong connections with another school in the MAC, contacted the conference and shared with them what he had learned. It was only a matter of months before the league handed Marshall the proverbial pink slip.

Players getting paid in dollars and favors were not the only misdeeds. The program was also plagued by irregularities involving financial aid and federally insured student loans. My experience with favors and money was zero. I never got free dry cleaning and never received any unmarked envelopes with $100 to $200 cash inside, which I'm told was the standard pay in those days. What I do know about is the loan I assumed as a freshman.

During preseason practice, a day was set aside for most of the freshmen to go downtown to one of the banks. I can't remember exactly how many of us went, but it was quite a few, including my two roommates. There were enough of us in the building that it resembled a Friday afternoon when banks are crowded with people standing in line to cash their paychecks. As far as I know, most of us got $1,500 loans. I don't remember spending much of that money on school-related items unless it was something like notebooks, pens, and pencils. I do not recall making any payments for tuition, room and board, or books. As far as I was concerned, the loan was really spending money, which I used mostly to buy clothes, record albums, and off-campus meals.

With all the talent Perry Moss assembled that first year, it still causes me to wonder about the what-ifs.

- What would have happened if everybody on that freshman team had stayed?
- What would have happened if there had been no recruiting scandal and Moss had kept his job?
- How would things have turned out if the plane crash had never happened?

- How much further along would the program be if Moss could have added other recruiting classes to further enhance an already talent-rich pool of players?

Given the Herd's dismal varsity record from 1965–1968, the success of the 1968 freshman team guaranteed that wholesale personnel changes were imminent. Upperclassmen, for the most part, did not figure prominently in Moss's game plan. The annual varsity-alumni game of 1969 provided undeniable confirmation of the much-anticipated overhaul. Nineteen of the starting twenty-two players on offense and defense came from that undefeated freshman team.

With so many newcomers named as starters, it seemed like this could be the start of a wonderful winning tradition. If this group remained intact, Marshall had the makings of what could have been a super team by the time the freshmen reached their senior season. And just maybe we would have been good enough to win the MAC and get an invite to the Tangerine Bowl. That would have been a special treat for me, since that bowl game was played in Orlando, Florida, which was roughly a three-hour drive from my home in Jacksonville.

Prior to the start of spring practice that year, there was potential for trouble on the horizon. Most of the black freshmen were not happy about the scholarship situation. We came to Marshall with the explicit promise that we would earn a scholarship when we made the team. That had not happened by the start of the spring semester, so there was talk about boycotting spring practice as a means to get that matter settled.

In our minds, we had sufficient leverage to help us get what we wanted. After all, we were the catalysts that would spark much-needed change for a floundering program. As a team, we had every reason to believe that the best was still yet to come. It was clear that black athletes would get substantial playing time under Moss. Marshall needed better athletes to compete and win. In this case, most of the top players coming in happened to be black.

Staging a boycott was not a matter of the players paying lip service to the idea. After much discussion, though, we decided against it. Instead, we opted to let our play on the field do our talking for us. In the end, things worked out for our best interests. We got those scholarships.

All of us were sold on Coach Moss's ambitious plan to upgrade MU football. And we were certain that it wouldn't take that long. Attracting enough football talent was never an issue. A fairly quick turnaround would have been quite a coup, when you consider the state of Marshall University athletics when Moss arrived on the scene in January '68. Football was secondary, and that's putting it mildly.

In contrast, basketball was the center of the school's sports universe. The Thundering Herd consistently attracted its share of top-rated recruits, which included a few high school All-Americans. Memorial Field House, the school's home arena, was filled close to capacity most of the time. Fan interest was intense.

During this era, the Herd made back-to-back appearances in the National Invitational Tournament and advanced to the semifinals one year. Back then, the NIT was a lot more prestigious than it is now. By 1970, Mike D'Antoni, today's coach of the New York Knicks, had emerged as a silky smooth point guard in his sophomore season at Marshall. After college, he played professionally in the National Basketball Association and in Italy prior to coming back to America to start his NBA coaching career. Even though D'Antoni was a highly skilled assist man and scorer, he was not Marshall's premiere player.

It was Russell Lee, a sleek forward who closed out his college career as an All-American in 1972. The Herd finished the season ranked twelfth nationally in the final polls. Russell, six feet, five inches tall, was the No. 1 draft pick of the Milwaukee Bucks in the 1972 NBA draft. The Bucks, who had won the NBA championship the previous season with Kareem Abdul-Jabbar and Oscar Robertson, were so high on Russell that they took him ahead of their other first-round pick: Julius Erving of the University of Massachusetts. "Dr. J" never suited up for the Bucks. Instead, he started his Hall of Fame career with the Virginia Squires of the American Basketball Association.

Chapter Two

Season of Challenges

I spent the whole time at home during the summer of '69. This was the close-out year of a topsy-turvy decade, and the late '60s were especially turbulent. The assassinations of Dr. Martin Luther King, Jr. and Bobby Kennedy produced widespread feelings of despair that cut across all color lines. The escalation of the Vietnam conflict and the increased frequency of war protests on college campuses dominated newspaper headlines and television newscasts. The struggle for civil rights continued, but the popular sentiment among the black masses started to change to some extent. "Say it loud, I'm black and I'm proud" was just as much of a catchy slogan as "We shall overcome." In the meantime, the women's movement gained added momentum by shining the spotlight on gender inequality. The hippies and their accompanying drug culture were fixtures on the American landscape. With so much going on in society, you couldn't help but be aware. For me, though, football remained the center of my world.

Since I didn't stay in contact with anybody in Huntington over the summer, I was completely oblivious to the storm clouds hanging over the football program. When I returned for preseason practice in August, I went speechless for several minutes after hearing the news that Marshall got busted by the conference and the NCAA.

I checked in at my dorm late in the afternoon and rushed over to the football office. The only person around was Pete Kondos, the head coach of the undefeated freshman team who became the defensive coordinator for the varsity team in the spring of '69. Kondos had come in to clean out his office after being fired because of the football program's numerous infractions. We talked for a few minutes in the hallway and he briefed me about the state of affairs concerning the team. When he finished, he wished me well and said good-bye.

Moss wasn't relieved of his coaching duties until late August. As a result, school officials were forced to move quickly to fill that vacancy. Two days before the start of preseason drills, Rick Tolley was named as the interim coach. Tolley himself was still new to MU at the time. He joined Moss's staff as a defensive line coach in the spring of '69. Most of the players didn't know much about him, other than he had been an assistant at Ferrum Junior College (Virginia) the previous season when Ferrum won the national junior college championship.

What I remember most about Coach Tolley from that spring was how hard he worked the defensive linemen. Every time I looked around, I'd see those guys gasping for air as they finished running forty-yard dashes. Little did the rest of us know that we'd get a lot of the same in the weeks to come after Tolley was given the reins to run the team. Rick Tolley was not one of those shout-you-down types. Being verbally abusive was not his style. He had a quiet but fierce demeanor about him. You *knew* that he did not play games, he had no favorites, and he worked everybody—*hard*. By any and all standards, he was a tough taskmaster. He made sure that conditioning was never an issue. We were always running series after series of wind sprints.

The severity of Marshall's transgressions had serious repercussions. The Thundering Herd's roster shrank dramatically. For spring ball, there were eighty-three players on hand. When fall practice started, the varsity had only forty-one players. It was a substantial drop-off in manpower. In spite of the mass exodus, there were others, like myself, who decided to stay. Since I was on scholarship and in the starting lineup, there was no compelling reason for me to leave. Based on all the dramatic changes that took place in such a short period of time, those of us who returned should have sensed that the upcoming season would be radically different from what we experienced as freshmen.

One of the most critical losses from the freshman team was Ron Mickolajczyk, an offensive tackle from New Jersey. In my eyes, Mickolajczyk (pronounced MICK-o-LANjik) was a vastly different breed of athlete. "Mick" was six feet, three inches, 250 pounds, and all muscle. One of the local sportswriters tabbed him as "Hercules."

I had never seen a guy that big who walked on his toes. Maybe that explains why he consistently ran 4.8 seconds in the forty-yard dash, a cheetah-swift clocking for an offensive lineman. "Mick" came back for preseason practice but stayed just two days before transferring to the University of Tampa, where he became a three-year starter. Ron played two seasons with the Toronto Argonauts of the Canadian Football League and then played four more seasons with the New York Giants.

Even with Moss and some key players from the freshman team no longer on board, the 1969 version of the Herd was much better than the varsity from the year before. But it would take a while before the Marshall faithful could bask in the glow of watching their team win a few games by season's end.

The year 1969 was college football's centennial. The first college game ever played was between Rutgers and Princeton in November 1869. To commemorate the occasion, the National Collegiate Athletic Association distributed football-shaped decals nationwide for college teams to put on their helmets. The multicolored decal was blue with red trim, and the number "100" (in white type) was framed by a football. Players on every team also received a certificate acknowledging their participation in college football's one-hundredth season.

In my opinion, the team's headgear for that season was hopelessly bland. Instead of a school insignia, jersey number, or mascot—artwork that typically appeared on the side of the helmet—the only graphics placed on Marshall's milky-white helmets were those centennial decals and jersey numbers in small type on the back of the helmet.

In the '69 season opener, Marshall's sophomore-dominated squad played like rookies in a 27-14 road loss at Morehead State University (Kentucky). For those of us who were sophomores, it was our first varsity game—and it showed. There were a plethora of mistakes on both sides of the football that night. The Herd was flagged for 180 yards in penalties, which still stands as a single-game school record more than forty years after the fact.

Some news accounts of that game zeroed in on Marshall's young secondary getting torched for 243 yards and four touchdowns. A large chunk of that yardage came on short *check-off* passes to the running back in the flat, which was a "soft spot" in our zone defense. We never made the adjustment defensively and Morehead State took full advantage all game long.

I did come up with one drive-killing interception in the second half: a midair take-away that turned out to be the first and only interception of my college career. In the fourth quarter, I added to our mountain of miscues when I attempted to get a quick jump on a pass to the flat. In my eagerness to make a play, I left my area of the field open. My mental lapse caused a blown coverage, which enabled the Eagles to score the go-ahead touchdown.

It was bad enough that we didn't play up to our capabilities against Morehead State. But even worse was that we had practice on a Sunday afternoon after playing a game on Saturday night. I wasn't sure what to expect. We went through our usual warm-ups and drills and it appeared that we would head to the showers after about forty-five minutes on the field, which turned out to be wishful thinking.

Before we would leave, all the players were divided into groups according to position and we started running forty-yard dashes. We lined up and broke into a sprint when Tolley blew his whistle. Then we'd turn around, line up again, and take off at the sound of another whistle. Back and forth we went. We were not allowed to rest between sprints. It still boggles my mind that we ran so much *the day after* playing a game.

As we continued to run, I looked around and saw that we had attracted a small audience. I saw ten, maybe fifteen, students who lived in the dormitory located across the street from the practice field watching us from their rooms. When we finally finished, all the players were dog-tired. We ran *forty-four* all-out forty-yard dashes—that's a mile's worth! Forty-four was the official count, according to Bill Redd, a fellow student and friend of mine. Bill, who was not an athlete, never explained why he started keeping count. Guess he had a feeling that after losing to Morehead State the way we did that we'd probably get some extra work when we went to practice.

There was a lot more agony than ecstasy for most of the 1969 season. By late October, we were 0-6. In the meantime, Marshall had a twenty-seven-game losing streak dating back two seasons and was on the verge of setting a new NCAA record for consecutive losses.

As players, we realized that like it or not, Herd football was synonymous with losing. I remember several instances that provided indisputable evidence of that ugly truth. On road trips, we'd frequently see homecoming queens and floats when our team bus arrived at the stadium. Teams do not schedule their toughest opponents for homecoming. Of all games, nobody wants to lose at homecoming and spoil the festive atmosphere of the celebration. Given those facts of life, it's no wonder that Marshall turned out to be everybody's opponent of choice for their homecoming games.

We should have beat Morehead State in the opener, but we didn't. We came tantalizingly close to beating Northern Illinois, but ended up losing 18-17 on a late field goal. The rest of the games up to that point in the season—Toledo, Miami (Ohio), Western Michigan, and Louisville—ended as predicted with lopsided losses. With four games left to play, team morale wasn't exactly soaring. The way things had been going, the possibility that we might finish the season winless seemed very real.

The most physically painful loss came against the University of Toledo. Toledo is my birthplace, and one of my uncles lived there. I never knew much about the city because I only lived there a couple of years before moving to Florida. In every sense, the Toledo game was a game of hard knocks. The Rockets had this beefy bruiser of a fullback: Charles Cole. He's what I call one of those wide-load runners at 230-plus pounds. On one play, Cole broke free at the line of scrimmage and headed toward the sideline.

As a defensive back, you like it when a big back decides he can outrun you to the corner. A smaller, swifter defender has an easier time of going low and taking a big man's legs away from him. That's how I was taught to tackle when I started to play the game. *The bigger they come, the harder they fall.* That was the mantra we used during my sandlot football days as a youngster.

But this time, I forgot all about what worked on the playground and I went after the big fella. Cole turned upfield and we collided at the sideline. I hit him chest high, linebacker-style, and took him down. What happened next was a telltale sign of who got the best of it. Cole sprung to his feet quickly. So did I, but I didn't walk away like I was ready for more. Stunned by this stabbing pain, I felt like I had been smacked in the neck with a two-by-four. I found out later that it was a pinched nerve, a nagging injury that players learn to live with.

When I came off the field, the pain was so excruciating that I took my helmet off. I wasn't aware of it at the time, but a school newspaper photographer zeroed in on my bout with agony, and the snapshot he took ran in *The Parthenon*. The photo caption referred to Marshall's agony of defeat. Losing had nothing to do with that particular moment. Intense pain had everything to do with it. It took nearly two years *after* I quit playing football for the pain in my neck to finally stop.

I was my own worst enemy that season. Lack of consistency prevented me from getting more playing time. I'd start one game, play poorly, and then sit the bench for a few games. At midseason, I turned in one of my better performances in a 48-14 blowout loss at Western Michigan University. I didn't start but played the entire second half and finished with eight solo tackles. That's a lot for someone who plays safety, a position that's the last line of defense.

Marshall's defensive backs were very busy that day. Starting cornerbacks Larry Sanders and Nate Ruffin played the whole game and ended up with fifteen unassisted tackles apiece. The fact that our secondary had so many tackles was a clear indication of how badly we were mauled at the line of scrimmage.

Next on the schedule was an away game at the University of Louisville, and I was back in the starting lineup. Lee Corso, who is now a college football analyst on the ESPN television network, was the Cardinals' coach at the time.

My status as a starter, however, was short-lived. The Louisville game turned out to be the absolute lowest moment for me as an athlete. The third quarter wasn't even halfway over before I lost my starting position *again*, and I had no one to blame but myself.

It's a play I'll never forget. Louisville running back Jim King caught a pass from Gary Inman coming out of the backfield. As I came up to make the hit, I had a flashback from the Toledo game when I injured my neck after making a tackle. I was unable to block out the memory of the pain I suffered from that hit, and I didn't want to relive that moment again.

King wasn't nearly as bulky (around 195 pounds) as Toledo's beastly fullback, but the memory from that collision in the TU game would not go away. I was not at full speed when I made contact, so I wasn't able to deliver enough of a blow to take him down. It was a weak effort on my part, and King bowled me over around the thirteen-yard line on his way to a thirty-four-yard touchdown.

It came as no surprise when I was banished to the bench for the rest of the night. Marshall lost 34-17. It was a long and lonely bus ride back to West Virginia. Yes, I was embarrassed. But eventually I got over it.

Ironically, it was Marshall's homecoming that set the tone for a desperately needed turnaround. On paper, it didn't seem remotely possible that the Herd had any chance of pulling off a shocking upset of Bowling Green State University. History favored the Falcons, who had not lost to

Marshall in fourteen years. The seeds for surprise were sown in the days leading up to the homecoming game. The slogan for week—"Stop the streak"—captured the imagination of students and townspeople alike. For the first time in a long time, there was genuine excitement about the possibility that the Thundering Herd could actually win a game for the first time in more than two seasons.

The anticipation of victory was evident in every practice that week. Everybody was tuned in to having good practices, which typically leads to playing well on Saturdays. The dorms and many of the fraternity and sorority houses were adorned with signs of encouragement for the Herd to whip the Falcons. Late in the week, a bonfire pep rally was held at the intramural field located near the center of the campus. A crowd of around 500 people showed up for the event.

The game itself was fun to watch, even though I didn't get to play one down—not even on kickoffs or punt coverage. Our defense allowed over 400 yards but delivered when it really mattered with two interceptions and five forced fumbles. In the cold, wetness, and mud, Marshall pounded its way to a 21-16 upset win. In spite of the slosh, puddles, and potholes, fans swarmed the grounds at Fairfield Stadium to congratulate the players.

Weather conditions for Homecoming '69 made it easy to determine who played and who didn't. Since I sat the bench, my uniform was spotless, except for my cleats, which were packed with mud from taking part in warm-ups. After the game, I took some good-natured ribbing about not getting any playing time, but I didn't care.

Well, that's what I told myself.

One my buddies suggested that I should have flung some mud on myself to give the appearance that I had played. That would not have happened. I had way too much pride for that; I didn't see any use in trying to fake people out. Even though I didn't play, I was thrilled that we finally got that long-awaited breakthrough. We avoided the distinction of being the team that led the nation in losing.

As things turned out, the Bowling Green victory set the stage for a magnificent run in which Marshall closed out the season by winning three of its last four games.

After seeing little or no game action for three consecutive weeks, I was ready to get back on the field for the season finale against Mid-American

Conference title contender Ohio University. I didn't start, but I did get some meaningful playing time, mostly on passing downs.

This game had a memorable ending. Down 24-7 at halftime, Marshall roared back to take a 35-31 lead with a little over a minute left to play in the contest. Ohio put together a frantic final drive and had the ball inside the Herd's five-yard line. It was a goal-line situation, and I was pulled out of the game and replaced by starting safety Kevin Gilmore.

Watching from the sideline, I had a gut feeling the next play would be a pass to the tight end. I kept repeating: "Watch the tight end! Watch the tight end!" Perhaps nobody thought I knew what I was talking about. As a former quarterback, I was certain it was the right play to call. Running the ball was the safe approach for short yardage, so a pass play would most likely catch the defense by surprise.

Sure enough, Ohio quarterback Steve Skiver took the snap and fired a quick pass to the tight end on the right side. The usually sure-handed Gilmore was in position to make the game-saving interception near the goal line, but the pass ricocheted off his chest and fell to the turf. The Bobcats still had enough time to run another play, and they scored with five seconds remaining on Paul Kapostasy's short plunge. Ohio University escaped with a 38-35 victory.

The game's closing moments provided great theater for the fans. For the losing team, the aftertaste of defeat was comparable to sucking a barrelful of lemons. Two highly questionable pass interference calls on Ruffin on that final drive literally gave the game to Ohio on a platinum platter.

It's interesting to speculate, but the bottom line is that no human being will ever know what would have happened had I stayed in the game. It's not that Kevin had bad hands. He played running back and tight end before being switched to defense. Who knows? Maybe I would have missed the interception too. But usually you come up with the interception when you know who the quarterback is looking to throw to. And I knew where the ball was going. I expected it. Just call this another case of the what-ifs.

Sometimes I think that had I been on the field and made the interception, it might have caused me to change my mind about quitting the game. Had that occurred, it's quite possible that I would have played ball the following season.

For me, October 1969 was a pivotal time. Football had become a see-saw proposition with a lot more downs than ups. What it really came down to was whether I really wanted to continue playing this game. At one point earlier in the season, I became so despondent that I purposely missed a few practices and seriously considered putting the pads away for good. I dreaded going to practice. I didn't want to put in the necessary time to make myself a better player. The desire wasn't there anymore. There was no way I could fake it; I wouldn't want to. Nobody pressured me one way or the other in my decision making. In the final analysis, I opted to return for the remainder of the season. In doing so, I could honestly say to myself that I finished what I started.

I don't recall exactly at what point in October that I reached a decision about the 1969 season being my last. I played in six games and started three times that year.

Even though the Ohio game was my *last hurrah,* my love for the sport had not diminished. Still, I was keenly aware that the searing passion to compete was noticeably absent. Without that gnawing hunger to push me, there would be no full commitment, and that just wasn't good enough. At that juncture, I figured it was best for me to focus my energies on improving my grades and graduating.

My college football career wasn't what I had hoped it would be. And I have to admit that I rarely agreed with my position coach when I played varsity ball in '69. Frank Loria coached the defensive backs and he relentlessly bombarded our thinking with one message: *"If you do the little things, the big things will come."*

Loria was an All-America safety at Virginia Tech University as a senior in '67. He played in the same secondary with longtime Virginia Tech coach Frank Beamer. Loria was as close to being a contemporary of ours as anyone on the coaching staff. When Tolley brought Loria onboard, he hadn't been out of college for that long, which meant he wasn't that much older than any of the players. Coach Loria and I didn't see eye to eye, but he was *on point* about that constant message that none of the defensive backs would ever forget. In my career as a journalist, I've learned that paying attention to detail, learning your craft, and proper preparation make a world of difference. It's often the difference that separates the average from the excellent.

My days as a Marshall athlete also provided opportunities for me to learn how to constructively deal with frustration and failure. To overcome adversity, it's necessary to work through difficulties while maintaining the confidence to know within yourself that success is achievable. Most of all, you should never be satisfied with the status quo if your goal is to improve your current status.

Tackling was the major issue I had with Coach Loria. Defensive backs weighing 160 pounds like me generally had a tough time taking down 230-pounders the way he wanted it done. Loria loved that textbook-style hit where the defender launches head first into the runner's chest and then drives the runner to the turf. Coach demonstrated the technique in practice but followed up by showing us how he did it when he played in college.

The film clip we watched often was from a game between Syracuse University and Virginia Tech. Jim Nance, the bull elephant fullback from Syracuse, took a handoff inside the five-yard line and was headed to the end zone. Loria, who was five feet, nine inches, 175 pounds, met Nance head-on and stopped him cold for no gain.

Couldn't argue with what I saw on the film. It just went against everything I'd ever been taught when I learned to play the game on the playground. I was always the youngest player on the field playing against kids who were three to four years older. They always told me this: "I don't care how big a man is. If you take away the legs, he's going down."

I never embraced Coach Loria's way of tackling, but there was no way for me to avoid it. Every day in practice, we'd have head-on tackling. I will say one thing for those drills: all that heavy hitting really developed the neck area. I had one of those football *bull necks* and didn't really notice it until I went home for the holidays when everybody kept talking about it.

Chapter Three

Chilly Racial Climate

There weren't any racial tensions on Marshall's football team in 1969. Blacks and whites got along just fine. But away from the games, practices, team meetings, and study halls, it was a much different scenario.

At best, socializing among the black and white players was minimal. You wouldn't see any black players going to any parties hosted by the white fraternities and white sororities. Likewise, you'd never see any white guys showing up at a hotel or house party thrown by black folks. And it didn't matter if the party's location was near campus or in the heart of *the hood*. That's just the way it was. Blacks and whites seemed to be comfortable with that. Nobody felt the need to come out of their cultural comfort zone. Of course there were a few blacks and whites who intermingled frequently, but it wasn't commonplace. After all, this was Huntington, not Greenwich Village.

The late '60s marked the arrival of the first wave of black athletes coming to Marshall, which before then didn't have many black students. The school started to recruit more blacks for football and basketball.

At the same time, there was another movement taking place not only at Marshall but also at other colleges around the South. Up until then, it was standard procedure for black folks to enroll at historically black institutions. But even that was starting to change as a greater number of blacks *who were not athletes* opted to attend predominantly white schools. This trend was set in motion, in large part, by the desegregation of the public school systems at every grade level in the Deep South. With more blacks attending mainstream schools, there was bound to be some uneasiness among the races. There were a lot of whites who had never been around black people before, and vice versa. So it was inevitable that, at some point, there would be incidents that would spark racial unrest.

Macie Lugo encountered racial bigotry at Marshall before she moved in to her assigned dorm room in August '69. Classes had not even started yet. Macie, a black freshman, was weary and worn out. Her arrival on campus was delayed after the station wagon she was riding in broke down and needed to be repaired. It took several hours for the repairs to be completed. It wasn't until after ten o'clock at night that she finally reached her destination.

Macie got off the elevator on her floor with two black men carrying her luggage. As they walked down the hall looking for her room, they noticed two white girls coming from the opposite direction. As they approached Macie and her companions, the white girls started to talk loudly—apparently on purpose—so that Macie could hear the conversation.

"*I bet you that's your roommate,*" *the first girl said.*

"*If it is my roommate,*" *the second girl responded,* "*then I'm moving out.*"

Sure enough, the white girl moved out just as she promised.

"That," said Macie in an interview, "was my introduction to Marshall University."

*   *   *

The racial climate on campus was nothing more than a reflection of Marshall's surroundings. I discovered this in the most unexpected manner during my freshman year. Back home in Jacksonville, Florida, I grew up in the Episcopal Church, which was not the norm for black people living in the South. Most of the folks I knew were Baptist, Methodist, African-Methodist-Episcopal, or Holiness. In Jacksonville, there were just two all-black Episcopal congregations in the entire city. So I knew that since Huntington didn't have nearly as many blacks as Jacksonville that any Episcopal church I attended would most likely be all white. That didn't bother me. All I wanted was to stay with the denomination that I grew up with. No need for any changes. So I decided to visit an Episcopal church that was roughly a twenty-minute-walk from my dorm.

I walked through the front door and in a matter of minutes realized that I was the only black face in the place.

If it was possible for facial expressions to speak, I wonder what would have been said.

The people at this church acted surprised. It was like my very presence was offensive. I remember the pastor welcoming me. But I don't recall anyone else showing any warmth. This got me to thinking. What if I had showed up on a Sunday when Holy Communion was being offered? Now *that* would have been very interesting.

In the Episcopal Church, communion is handled quite differently from most other denominations. In administering communion, those who wish to partake leave their seats and kneel at the altar. The priest gives each person a piece of bread and each person drinks wine from the same cup. That's standard procedure in the Episcopal Church. Given the reaction of the members during my visit, I wondered if anyone would have declined to drink from the cup after I drank from it. This caused me to question if these people really adhered to the faith they professed. I never got to find out what might have happened. In spite of the pastor's efforts, I didn't feel welcome and I had no desire to come back.

*   *   *

In the late '60s, college campuses all across the country served as forums for public demonstrations, and Marshall University was no different. The fall semester of '69 provided an unexpected opportunity for Marshall's black athletes to actively engage in peaceful dissent.

Here's the story:

School administrators promised to give office space to Black United Students in the Student Union building. BUS needed an on-campus base of operations. Weeks and months passed and BUS, which had about a hundred members, was still without a home. The administration had not kept its word, which gave the impression that the school wasn't serious about delivering on its promises.

The formation of the Student Relations Center as the home for BUS would satisfy several needs and would be open to students of all cultures and racial backgrounds. The Center would do the following:

- Serve as a focal point for the cultural, social, and intellectual interests of black students;
- Be an on-campus agency to promote racial understanding;

- Fill that role as a university agency to handle charges of discrimination involving students and campus entities.

In response to the administration's lengthy delay in granting office space, the BUS leadership came up with the idea to stage a protest at the president's convocation, an event in which the school's president discussed the state of affairs of the university. This event was the Marshall equivalent to a State of the Union address given annually by the US president. Bob Wright, John Shellcroft, Howard Henderson, Diane Pegram, Lee Ernest McClinton, Don Ross, and Bill Dodson were the student activists who helped develop the BUS strategy to effectively voice our concerns.

The demonstration had its disappointing aspects. BUS didn't get nearly as much support from the black athletes as expected. In all, maybe ten black jocks (football and basketball players) participated. Many were reluctant to publicly support the protest. They didn't want to be connected with any activity that would be deemed controversial. Back then, black people who engaged in demonstrations were often referred to as "black militants," which had negative connotations. It was a term most closely associated with organizations such as the Black Panthers. In those days, the federal government viewed the Panthers as a subversive group. Nobody I ever talked to ever admitted this, but it was said that some of the black athletes feared they might lose their scholarships if they protested.

If that was true, not everybody agreed with that reasoning. Some of the black athletes felt quite differently. In our minds, this was not a time to sit down and keep quiet. Yes, playing ball on scholarship was our means to pay for our college education. But we were students too. And we saw no valid reason why black students shouldn't have access to the same resources, programs, and opportunities that other campus organizations had access to.

The demonstration was scheduled for Thursday in the early afternoon and the timing couldn't have been better. For the football players who wanted to participate, it meant that we had ample time to protest and still get to practice on time. About seventy-five black students arrived early at the scene of the president's convocation. We sat together as a group on the floor level, about fifty yards from the speaker's podium. Our positioning was done on purpose so that Marshall President Roland Nelson would be sure to see us as he delivered his keynote address. Wright (BUS president) and Shellcroft (a BUS cofounder) sat with other student leaders on stage.

A few minutes into Nelson's speech, Wright gave us a nod as he and Shellcroft approached the podium. Shellcroft interrupted Nelson's speech twice before he was allowed to speak. He explained the reasons for the protest as we rose up out our seats and stood silently with clinched fists raised high: the black power sign.

Before leaving, Shellcroft assured the near-capacity crowd at Gullickson Hall that black students were not hostile. The protest, he explained, was conducted to ensure that "our problem" would be made known to the entire university. When Shellcroft finished speaking, we tore up our programs and walked out in a peaceful manner. As the group departed, you couldn't help but feel the glares and stares coming from the audience. It was hard *not to take notice* of so many frowning white faces.

According to the student newspaper's account, Dr. Nelson didn't hesitate to address what the audience witnessed after the protesters left the building. "If you had experienced the things that they had, you might not be able to contain yourself either," the president said. The near-capacity audience applauded Nelson's statement.

Even though the demonstrators had vacated the premises, the protest was far from finished. The group maintained its single-file formation as we walked out of Gullickson Hall, which was located next to the football practice fields. We embarked on a twenty-five-minute march across campus to the main administration building known as Old Main. Some of us carried bricks, which may have been perceived by onlookers as a sign of belligerence. That was not the case. Those bricks symbolized the building space that BUS had been promised but had not received.

As we entered Old Main, our march became a foot-stomping exhibition. The echoing sounds reverberated throughout the building as people on the first floor came out of their offices to see what was going on.

Eventually we exited through the front door of the building. The destination was the bust of John Marshall, which was located at the front entrance to the campus. The school is named after John Marshall who served as the fourth Supreme Court chief justice of the United States (1801-1835).

As protesters arrived at the bust, those who carried bricks placed their bricks in a neat stack at the base of the bust. Larry Carter, a tight end on the football team and a Reserve Officers' Training Corps (ROTC) cadet, placed the last brick—painted black—at the top of the stack.

Later that semester, Marshall's administration made good on its previous promises and BUS finally got its long-awaited headquarters. The Student Relations Center, known affectionately as "the BUS station," was created to provide viable support programs for black students. Since its inception, the center has expanded its role to provide support services for women and international students.

By the start of the fall semester of '70, the university's Division of Student Affairs began to develop programming for the new center. Getting space in the Student Union was extremely gratifying. Through persistence and determination in dealing with the *powers that be,* BUS was now a full-fledged, fully recognized on-campus entity. It was sweet victory for the people of soul on Marshall's campus.

"We had our place, our gatherings, and our plans," said Bill Dodson, whose younger sister Angela was also active in BUS.

The rhythm and blues classic "We're a Winner" performed by the Impressions echoed our sentiments to the tee. It felt so good to see some tangible evidence that Black United Students was finally starting to gain full acceptance on campus. This just made me want to shout, "*Thank you, Lord, 'cause we're moving on up!*"

A little over a year after the BUS protest, November 13, 1970—*the day before the crash*—the racial situation on campus took a turn for the worse. Oddly enough, it was a sporting event that became a flashpoint for an ugly episode. Usually, athletic contests help bring people of different cultures together. In this instance, an intramural football game turned out to be a breeding ground for divisiveness and violence.

Black United Students played the all-white Kappa Alpha fraternity in the intramural football playoffs. It was a late-round match-up, either the quarterfinals or the semifinals—I can't recall which one. You'd think that, as the BUS head coach, I would've remembered that.

The KAs, one of the school's largest and most prominent Greek-letter organizations, were known for parading the Confederate flag at public functions. At this game, they stood proudly with the flag. It seemed like they had some sort of alluring allegiance to it. It was as if they were bound by some irrevocable oath to gleefully wave that flag, widely recognized by black folks as a symbol of unbridled bigotry.

A sizeable and boisterous crowd of about 300 people witnessed a fiercely contested battle. This was flag football, which in theory isn't supposed to be nearly as physical as tackle football. This was not a game for the squeamish.

On nearly every snap of the ball, you could see some flying elbows thrown by players on both teams. The explicit intent was to inflict bodily harm. The end result was a few facial bruises and a bloody nose or two. One of the BUS running backs was horse-collared by a defender and the white officials did not throw a penalty flag. It didn't help any that most of the refs' calls went in the favor of the KAs. Even though this was an intramural game, the intense tone was a lot like what I experienced when I played varsity ball. For me, the enjoyment came from being a coach and designing plays to get the most out of the talent we had. Did I miss playing football for the Thundering Herd? Nope.

As the game progressed, the BUS players felt they were getting a raw deal from the officials, which only added to the on-the-field hostilities. It might have been better if these teams had just put on the pads and dispensed with any niceties. The animosity was just as evident among the spectators. All game long, blacks and the KA frat brothers in the bleachers kept barking insults back and forth. Nobody remembers which side started it. But more importantly, this situation was about to reach a boiling point.

For black students, the Confederate flag represented a culture defined by slavery and racial hatred. Most of us had been exposed to racism in some form while growing up. That's why black students gritted their teeth every time we saw that flag being waved in celebration at home football and basketball games. Even though blacks showed restraint when it came to that flag, the KAs gave all appearances of being boastful whenever they brought out that flag, also known as "Stars and Bars." It was so clear that this white fraternity deliberately went out of its way to antagonize black people. Given those realities, it was not a matter of *if* an altercation would take place, but *when*.

The KAs had their own fraternity flag, but, for whatever reason, they preferred to display its Confederate counterpart at school events. It was like a symbol that the fraternity chose to embrace. "There hadn't been any (racial) strife until they brought that foreign element (flag) into the mix," Bill Dodson told me during an interview. "That flag had no business being there. It's a racist symbol, and it produced undue tensions."

After the game, supporters from both teams swarmed the field to talk to the players. As everyone started to leave, some KA pledges ran through a crowd of black students waving those Rebel flags. Nobody knows for sure whether the KA pledges were ordered by their "big brothers" to do what they did.

Blacks were in no mood to be subjected to any form of taunting. The reaction was predictable. A fight broke out between blacks and whites and those fraternity pledges got the worst of it. Whoever made the decision for those pledges to wave those flags in front of a group of blacks *had to know* they were inviting trouble. The net effect of such an action is the same as tossing a gallon of gasoline onto an already smoldering fire.

Order was restored after about forty-five minutes, but those pledges took some severe beatings from a riled-up group of blacks. Some of the blacks at the game that day were not Marshall students. A few weeks after the post-game free-for-all, I wrote a letter to the editor of *The Parthenon* calling for the school's Student Senate to pass legislation that would prohibit the waving of the Confederate flag on campus and at all university-sponsored events.

Three white male students from Marshall were injured in the Friday fights and taken to a hospital; I'm not sure if they were the same threesome who waved the Confederate flags at the end of the game. The city police filed a report but made no arrests. The incident was publicized the next day in the local briefs section of the Huntington newspaper. One student was admitted in satisfactory condition with a severe cut on his chest. The other two were treated for minor cuts and released.

The size of the crowd when the fight broke out was about the same as when the game started. The percentage of spectators by race was roughly 50/50.

One of the victims told the police that he was hit over the head with a bottle. The others reported that they were jumped from behind by five people as they were walking away from the intramural field. The police concluded that knives were used in the attack.

I didn't know of many black folks who routinely carried knives. In all likelihood, it was probably those *rake* combs that were used as weapons. The rake was used to comb the Afro, which was the popular hairstyle for blacks during that era. These combs were really cake-cutters. The teeth of those combs were comprised of twenty-one ultra-thin prongs made of metal. Each prong was about three or four inches long and was sharp on the ends. The prongs' sharp ends made it easier to comb your 'fro, but you could also do considerable harm, especially if you used the rake in a chopping motion to attack someone.

Once things finally calmed down at the intramural field, the crowd from the game left and went to the cafeteria to eat. Peace did not last for long.

Another skirmish broke out and two ladies (one black, one white) were going at it. Others managed to separate the two, and it's a good thing they intervened when they did. The black woman had a vice grip on the other lady's neck and was trying to ram her head through the glass panels that were part of the set-up for the tables being used for the salad bar.

With all the commotion, a group of maybe 150 black and white students left the cafeteria and ended up in the lobby area of the girls' side of the Twin Towers dorm, which is located adjacent to the cafeteria. By this time, the Huntington police had arrived on the scene.

The lobby was packed. You could not move in any direction without making bodily contact with another person. Members of Kappa Alpha and Pi Kappa Alpha (the Pikes), the two largest white fraternities at Marshall, stood on one side, fired up and ready to fight. On the other side of the lobby, a large group of black folks (students and townspeople) were just as angry and just as eager to respond in kind. The Pikes got involved because of family ties. One of their fraternity brothers and the white woman involved in the cafeteria fracas were blood relatives.

In the minds of the black male students, there was no reason for these white fraternities to do battle since the altercation in the cafeteria involved two females. When those frats banded together, it had the look of a group intent on extracting revenge. The black guys from Marshall and the community believed it was their obligation to protect the black woman from this show of force by white males. It's very likely that the white fraternities showed up in large numbers in the lobby for the same reason. Had it not been for the police who positioned themselves between these emotionally charged groups, and some rational reasoning from one of the cooler heads, there's no telling what might have happened.

In the meantime, the football players were leaving the cafeteria after finishing dinner. None were aware of the fight because they were seated in a private section that was cordoned off from the main area of the cafeteria.

One of the first players to enter the crammed lobby area was Larry "The Governor" Brown, a black defensive lineman. The Governor wasn't among the biggest who played on the line at five feet, nine inches and 230 pounds. But he certainly had a knack for carrying a conversation in a soothing manner. In this instance, his presence produced an air of calmness in the face of an imminently explosive situation. He was one of the *cooler heads*.

This natty dresser from Atlanta, Georgia, usually sported a stylish brim. He had a way of relating to everybody regardless of skin color or culture. It's hard to imagine anyone *not* liking him. Had he lived, it would not have surprised me if Gov would have carved out a nice career niche in the political arena.

At this moment, though, Larry Brown's persuasive skills were desperately needed. There wasn't much time for him to do very much. But in the few minutes he had, Gov managed to get his point across, which helped to avert what could have been a frightening chain of events. In a jam-packed lobby, I wasn't close enough to Gov to hear what he said. Whatever it was, people listened. And they responded by backing off from confrontation and allowing their anger to subside.

Bill Redd was close enough to hear what Gov had to say. He told me, "I remember Governor jumping in the middle (of the crowd) and saying, 'Break this stuff up!' He pretty much let everybody know that the first blow thrown would have to come through him. He ordered everybody to break it up and go home."

The police did their part to quell the disturbance, but they certainly got a little help courtesy of Larry Brown.

After Gov arrived at the scene, other players filed through the area, curious about what was going on. They couldn't hang around for too long; they had an airport-bound bus to catch. I remember watching my best friend Scottie Reese walk through the double doors of the lobby entrance to the outside. That was the last time I saw him and rest of the guys on the team.

Scottie wore a dark suit coat and a pair of pearly white trousers that he purchased from Eleganza, a mail-order operation widely known as the black fashion haberdashery of its day. The merchandise was strictly *city*. The only places you would find what they sold in those catalogues were the major urban locales, such as Atlanta, New York, Chicago, and Los Angeles—in other words, cities with a whole lot of black folks.

The Friday the 13th brawl fueled much anger and resentment among blacks and whites. There were major concerns as to whether black students could even walk around campus and feel safe. Rumor had it that the two white fraternities contacted members from other chapters and they were supposed to visit Marshall to help them settle matters with the blacks. That night, the word went out among black students that regardless of where we might go, we needed to be in a group to help assure our protection.

Still, I was worried. In my own mind, the rampant speculation about white fraternities seeking revenge against blacks was very real—especially in regard to the safety of Marshall's black female students. I couldn't help but think about my fiancée Earnestine Ross, who lived in an apartment building not that far from campus. Earnestine and her three roommates frequently walked back and forth from their apartment to different areas of campus nearly every night.

Prior to coming to Marshall, Bill Dodson had first-hand experience with racial run-ins. At that time, he lived with his parents in an otherwise all-white section on the east side of Chesapeake, West Virginia. Most of the town's blacks lived on the west side, and that's where Bill spent most of his time. To get home, he had to catch the bus. If he missed that last bus, he had to walk a couple of miles.

When Bill D. had to walk home, he'd get heckled frequently by whites as he attempted to hitch a ride. Being subjected to a lot of vulgar name-calling was typical. One night, a carload of whites yelled out the *n* word. Bill promptly responded by chunking a rock that caused a loud thumping sound as it hit the vehicle. Almost immediately, the car screeched to a halt, made a swift U-turn, and shifted into high gear to find Bill. They wanted revenge in the worst way. Bill charted a path to safety by running between houses as fast as he was able. He stayed low to the ground, making it difficult for his pursuers to see him. Bill, by the way, made it home in record time. He was very concerned that he and other black students might find themselves faced with a similar situation after those on-campus fights.

"There was apprehension on our part," he admitted. "After what happened on Friday, we didn't know how far things would go. So we got the word out that nobody should go anywhere alone. We felt this was a real threat in which there would either be retaliation or confrontation. The 13th *did happen*. It was real. It just didn't get the air play. It was never widely known exactly what happened after the game or in the cafeteria. All the (racial) tensions that were on every college campus in America, we were mirroring at Marshall."

Chapter Four

Unforgettable, Unbelievable

November 14, 1970: The night was damp and chilly with a steady drizzle and dense fog. Looking out the window from my fifth-floor room at South Hall dorm, the lights from street traffic were barely visible from a block away. The usual nighttime glow from the houses in nearby neighborhoods was nonexistent. Weather conditions reminded me of scenes from those old Wolf Man horror flicks shot in black and white. A full moon and faint-sounding howls in the distance were the only missing elements.

In piecing together the chain of events from that night, some things are still somewhat fuzzy. What I do remember is that somewhere between seven thirty and eight o'clock I started hearing murmuring coming from the dorm hallway. I was relaxing and looking forward to attending an off-campus party later that evening.

There was talk of a plane crash at Tri-State Airport. Even though I realized it was about time for the football team to arrive on its return trip, it still didn't register that Marshall might be involved.

Gina (Starling) Gunn had no doubts. The day before the crash, Gina, a seventeen-year-old freshman, visited her dad, who was the assistant athletics director at Marshall. Ed Starling made the team's travel arrangements and would've been on that flight, but he didn't go because of a death in the family. "I saw all the (travel) information on my dad's desk," Gina explained to me. "So *I knew* it was the Marshall plane."

Once it was confirmed that it was the MU football team, there was no immediate mention about survivors. That was good news. There was still reason to hope that this would not be a worst-case scenario. Without realizing it, I was already in denial. I refused to consider the possibility of fatalities.

About twenty minutes later, another news flash: even though the rescue crews at the scene were still working, it was highly unlikely that anybody survived. The unspoken expectation was that *somebody* had to make it, that there just had to be some people who suffered injuries but were still alive and only needed to be taken to a hospital for treatment and observation.

Not long after that latest news update, I got a phone call from my Aunt Ann who saw the news on television from three times zones away in California. Ann knew I played ball and she called my parents, convinced that I was more than likely on the plane. They assured her that there was nothing to worry about, that I wasn't playing football anymore. In the years following the crash, Ann and I never talked about our conversation from that night. But it's my guess that even though she talked to my parents, she wanted to hear my voice for herself and decided to call me anyway.

As a professor and black student program director at Sacramento State University, Ann was acutely aware of how typical it is for college kids to change their minds about different things and not tell Mom and Dad. As our hour-long talk continued, it was evident that she made contact for her own peace of mind. What still stands out most about that call is how she lamented over the loss of so many young people who would never realize their potential. None of the players were older than twenty-three.

Elsewhere on another floor in the same dorm, the pay phone in the hallway continued to ring for several minutes. Folks were frantic about making contact with the school to find out about the players who were on that flight. Chuck Landon, a sophomore, rushed from his room and answered the phone. Larry "the Governor" Brown's sister was on the other end. She wanted to know if her brother was alive or not.

Chuck was caught off guard. He didn't know exactly how to answer. He knew there were no survivors. Nevertheless, he was extremely hesitant. Should he be the one to give her the bad news, even though it was the truth? He remained indecisive and decided to give what he felt was a safe reply: "Well, nobody's really sure right now. Nobody's been identified yet."

Chuck did his best to maintain a reassuring tone of voice as he said good-bye. After hanging up, he started second-guessing himself right away. "I hated myself a little bit," he said. "I should have had more courage to tell her that her brother had died. Things were so overwhelming that night."

Macie Lugo, a sophomore, was dating Larry "Dupree" Sanders, a standout cornerback and Marshall's best defensive player. Macie, the school's black homecoming queen known as Miss Black Pearl, was in her dorm room at Twin Towers when she first heard the news bulletin on the radio: *"This is an emergency! There has been a plane crash at Tri-State Airport!"*

Macie let out a shrill shriek heard by every resident on her floor. In spite of attempts to console her, she was convinced that her worst fears had come to past. All that week, she couldn't shake the feeling that something would go wrong on that flight. "Right after I heard it, I told myself, 'Dupree is dead,'" Macie recalled. "It was the team's plane. I knew it in my soul. I remember asking myself if I could go on living without him."

At Pritchard Hall, Janice Cooley heard women screaming in a nearby hallway, but she had no idea why. Soon afterward, she got a message to go downstairs and take a phone call at the lobby desk. The caller on the other end, a girlfriend, wasn't sure how to approach her. Art Harris, who was Janice's boyfriend, was a passenger on that plane.

"Janice, heard anything about a plane crash?"

"What plane?"

"There's been a crash at the airport."

"You don't think that's *our* plane do you?"

"Well . . . it *could be.*"

"No way! No way! No way!"

Janice refused to entertain any notions that the football team might be involved. She was confident that even if there was a crash, it was not the Thundering Herd. Janice left the front desk and went upstairs to her room. The dorm mother knocked gently at the door and entered. In as delicate a manner as she could manage, the dorm mother broke the news that everybody onboard the Marshall plane had been killed. In an instant, Janice snapped. Totally consumed by rage, she responded by slapping the dorm mother in the face with an open hand. "I slapped that woman as hard as I could," she said. "The news was so painful. I told her she didn't know what she was talking about."

Those who lived near the airport recall hearing an ear-splitting sound when Marshall's plane exploded. According to reports, the impact was so great that it caused houses in the surrounding area to shake. The crash scene did not stay isolated for long. Less than thirty minutes afterward, people swarmed the area. It took the authorities nearly two hours to finally clear the site of friends and family members of the victims, the news media, and onlookers.

One of the most mind-numbing sequences on this horrible night involved the wife and three children of a local sportscaster who was a passenger on that flight. Despite the foggy conditions, they watched and waited for the plane to arrive as scheduled, but it never touched down on the runway. The DC-9 jet disappeared behind a hill. And then there was a brilliant flash followed by a mushroom cloud of black smoke, made visible at nighttime by the brightness from the explosion.

Predictably, the plane crash produced an emotional tsunami of mourning and depression for everyone with any kind of connection to the school or the city.

Larry Isom heard about the crash and got a sick feeling in his stomach. Isom, a sophomore, was not an athlete, but he had more than a passing interest in Thundering Herd football. He and cornerback Bobby Joe Hill were best friends. In Isom's mind, it was unthinkable that Bobby, known to everyone as "Bee-Bop," might be dead. Soon after the news broke, Isom was among a group of twelve students who crammed inside two cars for the drive to the airport. Everybody felt the urgency to get to the crash scene as soon as possible.

When they got there, the main road was blocked off. The car Isom rode in pulled up beside one of the National Guardsman on duty. They would not be allowed to travel any farther. Before turning around and driving off, one of the students in the car insisted on gleaning more information from the guardsman. "Is this the football team's plane that went down?"

The guardsman responded with a company-line response. "I can't say. Right now, there's a lot that we just don't know."

Not satisfied, another student in the car spoke up. "Just tell us. Is it?"

The guardsman relented. "You all are going get me in trouble. I'm not supposed to be telling you any of this. Yes, it is Marshall's football team."

The reaction to the news that nobody wanted to hear didn't settle very well. Wailing and screaming combined with moans of anguish pierced the night air. As the car turned around to leave, Isom heard shouting coming from the other carload of students. Somebody knew about an alternate route that would put them closer to the scene. It was the only accessible way to get to that part of the mountain where the crash occurred.

One car followed the other down this narrow dirt road, which wasn't too far from the highway. When the two carloads arrived, they quickly realized they were not alone. One side of the road was littered with cars, trucks, and ambulances. The flashing lights from the ambulances and the steady beams from the headlights of the other vehicles aided visibility to some extent.

Isom got out of the car and noticed a group of nearly a hundred people running in one direction. Instinctively, he followed the pack and bypassed a lot of folks on the way. Nobody seemed to care about the numbing cold or the muddy terrain, which caused more than a few folks to slip and slide as they moved about. The foggy conditions didn't help any either. After running what seemed like a mile-long distance, Isom and the others turned off the road and ventured into the woods. Even though the area had been roped off by the emergency rescue team, it wasn't enough to keep people away. There were no state police, National Guardsmen, or volunteer firemen in the vicinity, so the crowd of onlookers continued to press their way through the dense woods.

It wasn't long before they came to a small hill. People started walking and running up this slightly steep incline. They were not prepared for what they saw when they reached the top: a front-and-center view of the Marshall plane lying at the bottom of the hollow. Debris and pieces of the aircraft were strewn about over a radius of about a quarter of a mile. Some of the wreckage continued to burn for several hours after the crash.

"After a while, we realized we weren't going to find anybody," Isom said. "It was time to go. The people I rode to the airport with had already left. To get back to the school, me and a friend of mine had to ride in the trunk of a car."

Back on campus, mass anxiety reigned. There was still no "official" word about survivors. Time inched along at a snail's pace. With every passing hour, it became more and more apparent that the unthinkable had occurred. Marshall had a major catastrophe on its hands.

At this point, I felt it would be best to distance myself from what was happening all around me. The speculation as to who might still be alive was not a topic I wanted to talk about. I needed to get out of the dorm. As I walked outside, folks seemed to be headed in one of two directions. The on-campus Christian Center was filled to capacity with students consoling one another. Gullickson Hall, the physical education building, served as a refuge. Gullickson, which was used as temporary quarters for relatives of the crash victims, was crowded with people who kept clinging to the hope that survivors would be found.

As for me, I was very uncomfortable about *any* ability I might have to comfort *anybody*. What was I suppose to say? How could I possibly be of any use to anyone when mentally I was in a daze? That's why I had no desire to hang around the dorm or any place else on campus that night. So I left campus and went to see my fiancée. As cold as it was, people were milling about on the walkways at her apartment complex. It wasn't until past midnight that the steady stream of visitors who stopped by to check in on Earnestine and her roommates began to tail off. There wasn't a lot of prolonged conversation. Mostly there were long periods of silence as we sat in the living room and watched television news updates. This was supposed to be a night to party. Instead, it was a night of unforgettable horror.

A sizeable crowd converged on one of the city's hospitals hoping and praying for the miraculous to occur. At the airport, a driver was placed on standby for the purpose of transporting injured people by shuttle bus to the hospital. In both cases, the waiting was in vain. By midnight, it was clear that there would be no need for those services.

Angela Dodson, the younger sister of Bill Dodson, first heard about the crash as she returned to campus after going home for the weekend. Angela, a fellow journalism major at Marshall, doesn't recall why she came back earlier than usual. It was around nine o'clock. The news—and the shock—were just beginning to set in.

The area around the dorm where Angela lived and worked as a resident adviser had a massive overflow of people, a lot more than you would normally see on a Saturday night. Mattresses, pillows, and bed covers were piled in heaps everywhere: on the steps, in the lobby, in front of elevator entrances, and people were bringing more of those items from upstairs to take over to Gullickson.

"I was aware of what had happened," Angela said, "but it took me a while to get a sense of what everyone was doing. It was a strange scene to see people throwing mattresses out (of their dorm rooms). As soon as I got on my floor, I heard screaming. It was a long night. I had thirty-two girls and everybody was crying. We had to take two ladies in for counseling that night."

According to news accounts, Gullickson Hall was frantic with activity. Doctors were on hand to treat frazzled students for shock. Athletic officials were on the phone lines trying to make contact with people who were supposedly not on that DC-9 jet. The coeds who weren't being treated, consoled, or counseled made themselves useful by passing out cups of coffee to students.

Cledis McQuay Hill called the South Hall dorm earlier that evening to get an update on her son Bobby. Even before Isom returned to his dorm, he knew he'd have to find a way to tell Bobby's mother that her son was dead. Isom was close to going into panic mode. This was the first time in his life that anyone close to him—friend or family member—had died. He wasn't sure what to say or how to say it. And since Bobby was so young (nineteen), it made things even worse. Isom and Mrs. Hill did talk on the phone that night, and he knew there was no way he could sugarcoat reality. He needed to clearly communicate the truth.

"Got any good news for me, Larry?"

Isom took a deep breath and spoke. "No, Mrs. Hill, I do not."

Bobby's mom sobbed uncontrollably. Isom could only listen, empathize, and hopefully say something encouraging that might comfort her in some small way. The only thing he could think of at the time was to provide assistance in gathering Bobby's personal effects or taking care of other matters that might need to be tended to at the school.

"If you need to come up here (West Virginia), I can make arrangements," he offered.

"There won't be any need for that," Mrs. Hill said. "Bobby's gone, so what's the point?"

Two of the school's assistant football coaches—Mickey Jackson and Carl Kokor—heard the news Saturday night while driving back from Pennsylvania after watching Penn State play Ohio University. Both were assigned to scout Ohio, the next opponent on Marshall's schedule.

Jackson and Kokor made repeated attempts to call Huntington, but all circuits were tied up. It took a few hours before they made contact with the Highway Patrol, which verified that the crash occurred and there was a possibility that there might not be any survivors.

Tired, sad, and stunned, the coaches got back in town around five o'clock Sunday morning. But instead of going home and getting some much-needed sleep, they immediately went to the football office. The first order of business was taking calls from family members of the crash victims to help bring some level of calmness to a chaotic situation.

Quite a few folks on campus woke up much earlier than usual on this particular morning. Usually a lot of students get in right before the break of day on a Sunday morning after partying the previous night. In this case, the night before was unlike anything that any of us had ever dealt with.

Chuck Landon, his roommate, and his friends were up early and made a beeline to the nearest newspaper dispenser, located one block from campus. He knew that if they got there before five o'clock when the delivery man made his drop-off, they were sure to get a copy of the Sunday morning paper that was sure to be sold out by nine o'clock. "When I got my copy and saw it in print, it made everything very real," he said.

I woke up around six o'clock that morning after falling asleep on the couch at my fiancée's apartment. As I walked back to the dorm, it was impossible to erase the memories from the previous night. This was a hard-to-swallow reality pill. The guys we had seen just two days earlier—the same guys we studied with, joked around with, partied with, and ate meals with—were gone, never to return.

I picked up the Sunday newspaper and read the front-page headline: "Marshall Team, Coaches, Fans Die In Plane Crash." In my head, I knew it was true. But emotionally, it was difficult to accept. I couldn't fully grasp the magnitude of what had happened. Quickly scanning all the headlines, I was shaken when I turned to an inside page that had a picture of every person who was on that flight. As I looked at the pictures, I could remember when most of these guys first came to Marshall.

The first person I looked for on that page was Scottie Reese, my best friend. He was to serve as my best man at my wedding in December. Scottie played outside linebacker and defensive end. We both came to Marshall in '68 and were starters on the freshman team. As sophomores, we were roommates on road trips. He didn't match up size-wise (six feet, two inches, 190 pounds) with others who played the same positions, but his field awareness and football IQ made him an exceptional player. Scottie would more than likely have had a career as an officer in the military. He was in Army ROTC at Marshall and was working toward earning an officer's commission by the end of his senior year of college.

As I continued to read and reflect, I found myself looking more at pictures of the players (both black and white) I was most familiar with—the members of the freshman team from '68.

- Bob Harris, a white quarterback, was versatile enough to play wide receiver and defensive back.

- Dennis Blevins, a black receiver, pushed me to the limit when we ran the 400 meters and the 4 x 400 relay on Marshall's track team as freshmen. Every day in track practice, I was determined to beat him in a quarter-mile race, but I could never do it. Dennis had stamina in abundance.
- Willie Bluford, a black running back, was a punishing inside runner who was moved to linebacker for the '70 season. I admired Bluford's work habits. He didn't have breakaway speed but had a knack for gaining the tough yards, and he rarely fumbled.
- Larry Sanders, a black cornerback. I'm glad that I never had to play against him as a receiver. I got a taste of what opponents faced during a scrimmage session. I lined up as wide receiver on his side of the field and ran a route where I had to come back several yards to make the catch. Out of the corner of my eye, I saw that I had gotten some separation from his coverage. I was open, or so I thought. When the ball arrived, so did Larry. He hit me so hard I thought I had blacked out momentarily.
- Roger Childers was a newlywed who got married eight days before the crash. He came to Marshall in '68 and was the only white player in the starting secondary on the freshman team. The next year, he played linebacker and then sat out the '70 season after undergoing major surgery. The year he sat out, he was the team manager. Roger had planned to return to competition in '71.

The enormous sense of loss was not limited to the football team and most of the coaching staff. There were Marshall athletic administrators on that plane, as well as a number of boosters who were prominent figures in the community—attorneys, doctors, business people, and civic leaders. Several folks, including two sisters who were Marshall cheerleaders, lost both parents that night.

In all, Southern Airways Flight 932 claimed seventy-five lives.

A day or so after the tragedy, several of Marshall's remaining football players expressed their desire to finish what their fallen teammates had started. After all, the season wasn't over; there was still one game left on the schedule. The only players left were those varsity guys who didn't make the trip because of injuries and members of the freshman team. They wanted to play Ohio as a tribute to their deceased teammates.

The players left behind held a meeting to talk about the immediate future. About thirty-five players, mostly freshmen, were in attendance. Reggie Oliver, the freshman team's quarterback, recalls the wide range of emotions displayed in that meeting and the varying opinions as to what they should do as a team. Some wanted to play; some didn't. As an outward show of solidarity, the players signed a petition requesting that they be allowed to play that final game to close out the season. They taped the petition on the wall next to Coach Tolley's office door.

"We felt the need to make a statement," said Reggie. "We wanted to let it be known that this is what we wanted to do, if we were allowed. Once everybody's emotions got settled, we thought about things more rationally."

The desire to play the season finale was an understandable knee-jerk reaction to dreadful circumstances. The intentions were honorable, but it was a bad idea. For starters, freshmen were not allowed to play varsity ball under NCAA rules. Plus, this decision never took into account that many of the players' funerals would be held the same day of that game and that people would want to attend those services. Not only that, but it's very unlikely that Ohio would've agreed to even play that game.

There was never a question about what the final decision would be.

Game canceled.

"That was very courageous," said Coach Jackson in an interview, referring to the team's petition to continue the season. "They thought it would make a statement. But with so much going on, there was no way that anyone could focus on putting together a team to practice and prepare for a football game that week."

You couldn't go anywhere in the city and not be reminded of what happened. The sentence on the marquee at a local Holiday Inn summed things up succinctly: *"The Lord Giveth, the Lord Taketh Away."* Around town, flags were lowered to half-staff. Front-door entrances to city government offices and places of business were adorned with funeral wreaths. Unless you were there, you could never fully comprehend the gravity of grief that engulfed Huntington, West Virginia, in the days to follow.

It wasn't uncommon to see written messages on store windows that expressed condolences to the families of the crash victims. The university, city, and county governments shut down for two days. Scheduled events for the region were postponed or canceled. Marshall resumed its regular schedule by midweek, but it was hardly business as usual.

The night after the crash, a memorial service was held at Memorial Field House, the off-campus arena where Marshall played its home basketball games. I knew well in advance that I would not be there. My feelings from Saturday night had not changed. The Field House was not where I wanted to be.

That's not how a lot of other people felt. There were few vacant seats in the stands or on the floor level at the Field House (about 7,500 attended). Dignitaries representing the school, the city of Huntington, and the state of West Virginia were present. The heaviness of the occasion was readily evident.

The classic hymn "O God, Our Help in Ages Past" provided a sense of hope and assurance for a community in deep mourning. People listened to words of comfort, hugged one another, held hands, and did whatever they could to help in sharing the burden of grief and sorrow. "Everything seemed so quiet," said Gina (Starling) Gunn about the service. "There was such a feeling of numbness."

I didn't say much of anything to my fiancée about Scottie. The three of us came to Marshall in '68. Earnestine was part of that initial wave of non-jock blacks who started attending predominantly white colleges located in the South at that time. Even though we realized that the crash did happen, it was like we both were frozen in a state of being *numbfounded*. No tears, no bawling, and no wailing. No escape from the inner turmoil that seemed to be everlasting. We consoled each other in silence, probably because we didn't know any better. The pain was so profound. Words could never adequately describe the depths of our despair. An encounter with Scottie—three weeks before the tragedy—remained fresh in our memories.

Scottie was among the first to be informed about our engagement and upcoming nuptials. Earnestine and I saw Scottie on a Saturday night near the Student Union building. He was headed to a house party that we had just left. We shared our news and Scottie agreed to be my best man. The wedding was set for December, right after the end of final exams.

It was still next to impossible for me to get a grip, particularly when I thought about those team members who came from the same hometown. Those "homies" grew up together and perished together. That was so sad to think about.

Cincinnati, Ohio, was home to four of the crash victims. Jim Schroer was the team trainer; the other three—Bob Harris, Jack Repasy, and

Mark Andrews—had played at Moeller High School. There was a similar situation in Tuscaloosa, Alabama, where four players, all teammates at Druid High School, were put to rest following a joint funeral held in the school auditorium. A huge crowd came to pay their final respects to Larry Sanders, Joe Hood, Freddy Wilson, and Robert VanHorn.

Bob Harris Sr., the father of quarterback/wide receiver Bob Harris, penned an inspirational letter of encouragement to the parents of players and others who were affected by the plane crash. The widely read letter was published in the local newspaper and Marshall's student newspaper. This letter was written from the perspective of what Bob, Jack, and Mark would have said if they were able. Here's an excerpt from that message:

> You have called us to Thy home in heaven and we come back home to Thee, our heavenly father. We pray to Thee, dear Father, for those we leave behind. Please bless them and give them the strength to uphold and keep safe the things we so dearly cherished while here on earth.
>
> Help our parents, brothers and sisters and all those so dear to know that we are with them through Thee now and forever. Grant them the blessing to accept Thy will as we have. Hold them close to Thy bosom, dear God, so that they may know joy—not grief, as we answer Thy call.
>
> Make them aware that our 20 years on earth were lived to the fullest, and were filled with love, warmth and happiness. We enjoyed an inner peace that comes from knowing we were loved by those whom we loved.

In the days immediately following the crash, there were still passengers who could not be positively identified. Bodies were burned beyond recognition when the DC-9 jet plunged into the side of a mountain at 160 miles-per-hour and exploded. Several days would pass before most of the bodies would be identified.

In many instances, parents and loved ones of the deceased players were forced to wait around before they could go into a dorm room and pack up personal belongings. Because of a Federal Aviation Administration mandate, they were prohibited from having access to players' rooms until each player who was an occupant of that room had been identified. In cases where deceased players were roommates, nobody could go in those rooms until both players had been properly identified. In the first few days following the crash, the South Hall lobby was flooded with the parents of players who were waiting to go in their sons' rooms. Some had to wait longer than others because of the time lapse in getting everyone identified. "It was like living in a funeral home," said Chuck Landon.

Scottie was one of the passengers who had not been identified immediately. So me and Sheila Callahan (another friend of Scottie's), went to his dorm room to look for items that might help in identifying him. As I rummaged through the suit coats, trousers, and jackets hanging in the closet, I thought back to homecoming and remembered how secretive Scottie could be at times. Everybody wanted to know who Scottie was taking to homecoming. And he seemed to get a lot of enjoyment in remaining tight-lipped about the matter. We'd all have to wait until homecoming weekend to find out.

"Who are you taking?" I inquired.

Scottie answered using a word I had never heard before. "Nunyah."

"What? Nunyah? What does that mean?"

"It means it's nun of ya' business."

The process of identifying all seventy-five passengers was exhaustive. The medical staff on hand had to rely on patches of clothing, dental records, fingerprints, key rings, watches, jewelry, and, in some cases, body parts to help identify victims. To help out with this task, it wasn't unusual for investigators to go by what friends and loved ones of the deceased remembered about the clothing the victims wore. In some cases, depending on other people's memories was the only means to help identify the charred remains.

All were identified with the exception of six players. Ten days after the crash, a joint funeral service was held at the Field House for Kevin Gilmore, Barry Nash, Allen Skeens, Tom Zborill, Dave Griffith, and Tom Brown. They were laid to rest at Spring Hill Cemetery in Huntington. The burial site serves as a lasting memorial to the 1970 team.

In the DVD *Return of the Thundering Herd*, Coach Kokor relives the most emotionally draining portion of that memorial service, which was held two days before Thanksgiving. During a scheduled moment of silence for the victims, one of Barry Nash's brothers left his seat and went to the front. In the stillness and quiet of the almost packed Field House, he ran from casket to casket and kept asking, *"Barry, is this you?"*

In the days immediately following the disaster, a school and community started going about the business of burying its dead. A television news director at one of the local stations commented how it became such a blur to cover so many services in a short time span—thirteen in three days.

One week after the crash, I was in Waco, Texas, to bid farewell to Scottie. I never considered taking the chartered bus that transported black students to several funerals in less than a week's time. (More on that in the next chapter.)

Yes, Scottie was gone, but he was still my best man. I know he had plans for Christmas vacation, but he let me know that he would delay his trip back home so he could be at my wedding. No disrespect to the other players, but for me, going to Waco was simply the proper thing to do.

This was personal. I felt a responsibility to go to Texas. As long as I had known Scottie, he had always proven to be trustworthy. Betraying someone's trust was something that Scottie Reese just didn't do.

During the funeral, I sat and stared at the jersey-draped casket and Scottie's portrait. That's when it finally dawned on me that No. 83 wasn't going to be around—ever. What did the preacher preach about? Don't know. What I remember most is the upbeat tone of that service. It was more of a celebration of Scottie's life as opposed to a mourning of his tragic departure.

Every time I hear the song "Fire and Rain" by James Taylor, I always think of Scottie. The image of him standing at the entrance of the dorm before catching the team bus to go to the airport is still fresh in my mind. I had no reason to believe that I'd never see him again.

Scottie had a certain wit about him, and Bill Redd, a fellow student who was not an athlete, got more than a few doses of it. Bill and Scottie became good friends when they joined a college fellowship group at one of the local churches. Bill remembers a Sunday when he and Scottie left campus in a hurry to get to church in time for the start of morning worship service. In Scottie's rushed departure, he forgot to put his socks on. Bill was quick to remind Scottie that he wasn't fully dressed. Their conversation went something like this:

"You can't be fully dressed if you're wearing shoes with no socks," Bill Redd said.

"The Lord doesn't look to see if I'm wearing socks or not," Scottie retorted. "He's much more interested in what's in my heart."

Assigning nicknames that never faded away was a Scottie Reese specialty. Whenever the team went to the dining hall, he noticed that offensive lineman Ed Carter could out-eat everybody. So, Scottie nicknamed him "Bodine," as in Jethro Bodine, the brawny character from the *Beverly Hillbillies,* a popular television show in the '60s. Bodine was known for his ravenous appetite. The guys on the team, however, knew that Marshall University's version of Bodine would never take a back seat to Hollywood's Jethro. For example:

- After cashing a paycheck from his summer job at the local steel mill, Ed headed to the grocery store and bought a lot of chicken. That night he cooked and ate two whole chickens in one sitting.
- Most Sundays while school was in session, Ed and two other players routinely pooled their money to purchase a twenty-one-piece barrel of Kentucky Fried Chicken. The school cafeteria closed early on Sunday afternoon, so students were left to fend for themselves when it came to eating dinner on Sunday. In those days, the KFC barrel had bigger pieces of thighs and breasts to go with the wings and drumsticks. Ed and his comrades split the barrel three ways, which means they each had enough chicken for two meals.

"Whenever we went to the training table, I'd eat more food than probably anybody else on that team," Ed said. "That's why he started calling me Bodine. Even after the crash, the name stuck with me, but it was Scottie who started it."

Even though it's been over forty years since the crash, people still remember Scottie. An anonymous writer posted the following blog entry about him on the *Herald-Dispatch*'s website. As part of the newspaper's coverage in the weeks leading up to the premiere of the movie *We Are Marshall,* readers were asked to share their memories from 1970. The movie's storyline focuses on the crash's aftermath, the football program's restoration, and the process the community went through to heal itself.

> *"Several of my friends were players on the 1970 MU football team. When I got news of the crash, the first person that came to my mind was a very special person, Scottie. He always talked about his Grandmother and how much he loved her. I'll always miss him."*

No facet of life at Marshall or the city of Huntington went untouched by the plane crash. You either had a close relationship with someone on that plane, or you knew someone who did. That's the norm in a close-knit college community. Marshall's football players were not housed in a separate dorm. They were assigned the same living quarters as regular students. It was the same way for meals. Because of that, there was a lot more interaction between athletes and regular students. A lot of meaningful personal relationships involving jocks and non-jocks developed.

That's why folks at Marshall were hurting in the worst way, especially on campus, which was also known as "the compound." You either knew the football players personally or at least knew *of* them. Everybody was overwhelmed by the bewilderment and anguish of the situation.

Looking back, there were a number of ironies about the air tragedy, widely acknowledged as the worst in American sports. A lot of the players were superstitious. They didn't like the idea of leaving town on Friday the 13th. It's been said that all during the week leading up to the road trip to East Carolina University, several players expressed their concerns. Some called home to tell their parents that they might not return. Others left personal belongings with their girlfriends.

The weather conditions during the daylight hours of November 14 created a mood of gloom around Huntington. It rained on and off all day long. The sky was so dark that you got the impression that the sun had gone into hiding indefinitely.

Meanwhile, the football team was forced to face its own depressing experience. The Thundering Herd suffered a heartbreaking 17-14 loss to East Carolina. Even worse, the game ended on a controversial call that went against Marshall. For the Herd faithful, it was a bitter defeat. Little did anyone know that the events that would occur *after* that game would compel everyone connected to the school and the city to forget all about football for the time being.

The night the Marshall plane went down will always be memorable for all the wrong reasons. Not only was it the first and only plane trip the team had for that season, but it was the first time that Southern Airways had ever flown into Huntington. Prior to that night, Southern had never had one of its planes crash in twenty-one years of doing business. The flight crew for this journey was an experienced group. Pilot Frank Abbott had been with the airline since its inception. The average length of employment for the other crew members was about six years.

The National Transportation Safety Board conducted an investigation to determine the cause of the crash. An NTSB panel of inquiry convened for a hearing in Huntington, which lasted three days. It took five months for the panel to complete its findings. The NTSB issued its final report in April 1972, but there is still no definitive explanation as to what caused the accident. The final report concluded this:

> The probable cause was the descent below Minimum Descent Altitude during a non-precision approach under adverse weather conditions, without visual contact with the runway environment. The Board has been unable to determine the reason for this descent, although the two most likely explanations are: a) improper use of cockpit instrument data; or b) an altimetry system error.

At the start of the '70 season, Marshall's team held so much promise. Fairfield Stadium, the Thundering Herd's home field, got a much-needed facelift with added seating and refurbished locker rooms. The playing field was converted from natural grass to AstroTurf. Marshall celebrated with a stomp-down victory in its season opener against Morehead State. This team had its share of studs, but the talent level wasn't quite the same once you got past the starting lineups.

As the season progressed, injuries and the lack of depth took a severe toll, and it really showed in the win-loss record. Entering the East Carolina contest, the Herd, 3-5 at the time, still had a shot at having a break-even season if it won its final two games. For a school that had finished on the downside of .500 for four consecutive seasons, ending the '70 campaign at 5-5 would have signaled humongous progress. Marshall posted a 3-6 record in its tragic season. In four of those losses, the *average* margin of defeat was 3.5 points.

Still, there's another ironic twist to this story: In early October, the Thundering Herd, along with other college teams around the country, paid homage to the Wichita State football team. Marshall observed a moment of silence during its pregame meal prior to playing Xavier University of Ohio. Wichita State flew two planes for a road game at Utah State and one of the planes crashed, killing twenty-nine people, which included thirteen players. Six weeks later, Marshall met the same fate. But compared to Wichita State, its losses were far more devastating.

In a way that was totally unexpected, the crash had a calming effect on race relations at Marshall. In '70, blacks comprised about 3 percent of a student-body population of 9,000. The football team's forty-seven-man roster for that season was 30 percent black.

Given what happened on Friday the 13th, many of us believed we were on the brink of a full-blown race riot at Marshall University. But before the night of the fourteenth ended, moods, emotions, and outlooks changed dramatically. Everybody suffered indescribable losses that transcended race and heritage. Nobody was thinking about any racial beefs. It was as if the Friday fights had never happened. Folks were too busy grieving and making plans to attend funerals. The recollections are still vivid in many people's minds, including a Huntington resident who submitted a blog entry for the *Herald-Dispatch* newspaper's website. The writer, who chose to remain anonymous, described how the crash played a pivotal role in black-white relations on campus.

> I remember the night oh too well. A number of us had been working to make sure a scheduled demonstration regarding racial intolerance on the campus would be peaceful. (Black student activists) Bill Redd, Bill Dodson and Angela Dodson were in dialogue with a number of white student leaders to avert any violence. The news came on and all talk of demonstrations, of race, of racial inequality stopped. We were a family, and we had lost so many of our family members. As a local resident, I not only lost campus friends and classmates, but members of the community. Not a day goes by that I don't think about them and my heart grieves.

In the months following the crash, Marshall's black student community was concerned that administrators would do everything in their power to punish all blacks who participated in the Friday the 13th melee. Within the black student community, some feared that a wholesale expulsion was in the works. During the spring of '71, ten black students were charged with assault and battery in cases filed in the school's student court.

There was an unspoken sentiment among black students that those who were being charged would most likely get railroaded right out of school. The make-up of the court was overwhelmingly white. Of the five judges (four students and one MU faculty member), only one was black. Nothing came of those charges, though. Not one black student was expelled.

"The intent was to kick them all out of school," said Bill Redd, who was the lone black judge on the Student Court that year. "They didn't prove their case, so we dismissed them all. They said (according to the charges) that it was all the black kids' fault. But the reality is that it was the white students who started it. I know because I was there. Right after the game, I remember a young man running down the middle of the field with a Rebel flag. That's what started the whole thing. People were beating people. I pulled one guy off another guy. It was a bad time."

The legacy of the team that perished goes way beyond wins and losses. It's my belief that this group had a divine calling to fulfill a greater destiny. The racial turmoil brewing on campus from those Friday fights was totally squashed because of what happened on the night of November 14. Racial and cultural differences really didn't matter anymore. The sorrow and shock were so complete that everybody forgot all about Confederate flags and racial heckling.

This wasn't a black thing.

This wasn't a white thing.

This was a death thing, and death does not discriminate.

Grieving people were too busy trying to make some sense of it all. So in ways that nobody could ever imagine, Marshall's '70 football team became an agent for peace between the races.

*　　*　　*

The 1970 team is generally recognized as the group that would have ultimately put Marshall on the college football map. What folks might not be aware of is that this team was comprised mostly of players recruited by Perry Moss in '68 and '69. There was some serious talent onboard, which included genuine NFL prospects. Here are some brief notes on the deceased players—black and white—who I believe would have played professionally.

- Larry Sanders-Savvy defensive back, strong on solo pass coverage, noted for delivering skull-busting hits. Big and muscular at six feet, three inches, 195 pounds. Excelled at providing run support.

Played cornerback in college, could have easily transitioned to safety at the next level.

- Joe Hood-Running back, had rare combination of size, sprinter's speed, and graceful moves. Reminiscent of Gale Sayers in his prime. Joe had little or no body fat at six feet, two inches and 200 pounds. Clocked at 4.3 seconds in the forty-yard dash running in tennis shoes on a gravel surface. Very fluid runner, exceptional receiver. A nightmare for any defender trying to take him down one-on-one in the open field. Could have done nicely in today's wildcat offensive schemes because he was also an accurate passer who could throw deep.
- Dennis Blevins-Big wide receiver (six feet, two inches, 190 pounds), legitimate deep threat with excellent hands. Tough to cover because of his leaping ability, physicality and speed (4.5 seconds in the forty-yard dash). Tireless worker kept himself in superb condition.
- Jack Repasy-Consummate possession receiver, speed was not his calling card. Compensated by running precise pass routes. Rarely dropped anything thrown his way.
- Art Harris-Smooth-talking running back known as "Broadway," played much bigger than his size (five feet, nine inches, 195 pounds). Highly recruited out of high school by most of the major colleges in the East and Midwest. He was expected to sign with the Herd in '68. Went to the University of Massachusetts instead and stayed for one season before transferring to Marshall. Rugged enough to run between the tackles, quick enough to make tacklers miss, swift enough to run past most defenders. Reliable receiver coming out of the backfield. Playing style similar to Ray Rice of the Baltimore Ravens.
- Marcello Lajterman-Placekicker, strong-legged sophomore routinely kicked field goals from fifty yards out in practice. Booted a forty-seven-yard field goal vs. Western Michigan in his only season of varsity competition. Soccer-style kickers were still relatively new to American football in the early '70s. If he had completed his college career, Marcello, born in Argentina, had the skills to rank among the best kickers of his day.
- Ted Shoebridge-Big-play quarterback, blessed with superb field vision and an uncanny sense of timing. Had scholarship offers

from many of the nation's top programs. Double threat as runner and passer. If he didn't make an NFL team, he would have found a home in the Canadian Football League because of his mobility.

Today, Marshall *represents* in the NFL. It's my opinion, however, that the school's pipeline to the pros could have materialized a lot sooner. If some of the players who died in the crash had lived and gotten the opportunity to turn pro, I'm convinced the Herd would have solidified its NFL presence long before Carl Lee, Troy Brown, Chad Pennington, Randy Moss, Byron Leftwich, and Ahmad Bradshaw came on the scene.

Lee and Brown are retired. Lee was a three-time All-Pro cornerback with the Minnesota Vikings, and Brown earned three Super Bowl rings as a wide receiver with the New England Patriots. Pennington has started at quarterback for the New York Jets and Miami Dolphins.

Moss, a record-breaking receiver and easily the most recognizable of all the former Marshall players, has a legitimate shot at making Pro Football's Hall of Fame one day. Leftwich quarterbacked the Jacksonville Jaguars for five seasons prior to moving on to Atlanta, Tampa Bay, and Pittsburgh (back-up QB when Steelers won Super Bowl XLIII). In his fourth NFL season in 2010, Bradshaw blossomed as one of the league's most productive backs with 1,235 rushing yards and eight touchdowns. Bradshaw turned pro after his junior season of college in 2007. As a rookie, he was a key contributor in the New York Giants stunning upset of New England in Super Bowl XLII.

The success of individual players at the professional level can have a profound impact on the success of a college program. Recruiting more top-grade athletes gives schools a better shot at winning consistently. That's especially critical for schools who are card-carrying members of college football's elite.

Year in and year out, the elites, such as the University of Oklahoma and Auburn University, routinely rack up championships and invitations to play in financially lucrative bowl games. The elite schools tend to fare better in the annual recruiting wars to sign the top players in the country. Loading the roster with gifted players is the difference-maker between teams that are good every once in a while as opposed to teams that are always ranked among the nation's Top 25. Most powerhouse teams rarely nosedive; they simply reload.

Football-wise, Marshall is not at the same competitive level as Louisiana State University or Michigan State University. But that doesn't mean that Herd football hasn't served as a springboard for NFL careers. When Marshall won national championships (NCAA Division I-AA) and bowl games after moving up to Division I-A (now known as the College Bowl Subdivision), the Herd was able to effectively stockpile talent, which enabled the school to consistently compete for championships. Marshall's on-the-field success attracted a greater number of players with pro potential. The end result: Herd football had its best years in school history.

Chapter Five

Homegoing Caravan

In the days immediately following the crash, the black student organization at Marshall—Black United Students—raised enough funds through private donations to pay for a chartered bus and airfare so students could attend services for the black players who perished. Some of the students went to New Jersey and to Texas. The others traveled by bus on a whirlwind trip that covered over 1,500 miles in five days. A group of fifty black students attended a wake and three funerals at four locales: Bluefield, West Virginia; Atlanta, Georgia; Tuscaloosa, Alabama; and Greenwood, South Carolina.

All aboard for the Homegoing Caravan!

In the tradition of the black church, *homegoing* is a time for jubilation. Yes, there is sorrow and sadness for those who have passed away from their earthly life. Yet there's cause for much joy because they have *gone home* to be with the Lord for eternity.

Gina (Starling) Gunn wanted to attend some of the funerals, but her parents ordered her to stay at Marshall. The Starlings had just returned to West Virginia after burying Gina's grandfather in Mississippi a week earlier. Gina had just turned seventeen, so her parents were concerned about her ability to cope with so much tragedy in such a short period of time. "When I told them I was planning to go, they said, 'No way,'" Gina said. "I understood where they were coming from. They felt it was in my best interest to stay. Still, I was extremely upset with them."

It's still amazing to realize that this trip was put together so quickly. Local ministers Reverend Charles Smith of First Baptist Church and the Reverend Dick Miller of Ebenezer United Methodist Church were instrumental in helping to facilitate the fund-raising effort.

To appreciate how quickly this all came together, consider the time line of events. The crash occurred on a Saturday night; by Wednesday, all but the most minor details had been worked out for the trip to actually take place. The chartered bus left Marshall's campus on a Thursday night for Dennis Blevins's funeral the next day in Bluefield. The group returned to Huntington early Monday morning of the following week after attending services for Willie Bluford in South Carolina—the fourth and final stop.

"At first it seemed like a wild idea," said Joe Bundy, a freshman who went on the trip. "No rational person would ever think it could be done. We had something like forty-eight hours to raise all this money to secure a bus for the trip south, airplane tickets for people to fly to Texas (Dallas and Waco), and travel money for students to go New Jersey. College students are idealists. We wanted to do whatever we could to make it happen."

The day after the crash, the school started assigning students to assist the parents and relatives of the players who died. When the relatives came to town, they were housed at a hotel near campus. Most had trouble getting any sleep. So they stayed up and talked, and talked—all night long. During one of those conversations, the suggestion was made to find a way for students to attend as many funerals as possible.

Bundy, who was assigned to assist Wilbert Wilson, father of tight end Freddy Wilson, found some relief from his grief in fulfilling his role. "Rather than think about how bad I felt about losing a homeboy (Dennis Blevins), my focus changed," he said. "I began to think a lot more about Mr. Wilson and what he was going through. This situation allowed me to be strong for the parent. Our role was to keep the parents lifted up. You didn't want to break down in front of them."

Getting fifty seats on the chartered bus filled was not a problem. There was a strong sense of obligation to go on this trip. Folks had a burning desire to pay their final respects. Nobody ever said it, but all of us knew it was the appropriate thing to do. Whites were not barred from the caravan. It just turned out that no white folks signed up to go. The school made sure that Marshall would be represented at every player's funeral by assigning various faculty and staff members to attend designated services.

Several campus organizations held memorial services for all the crash victims. But among the blacks at Marshall, there was a unique affinity because of skin color and culture. Call it a sign of the times. It was a time in which blacks were the small minority on white college campuses, but were very vocal in helping to pave the way for blacks' inclusion into every facet of student life. Marshall was no different. Back then, the black pride movement was at its peak. The soul hit "Say It Loud: I'm Black and I'm Proud" by James Brown became an anthem for blackness back in the day.

"Marshall was a very small community," said Angela Dodson. "There were only a few us (black students). To lose ten at one time was a big dent. In the midst of all the confusion and shock, we needed to do something active or proactive to try to process all that had happened and be part of it."

The most unique aspect of this trip was the kaleidoscope of emotions experienced by the passengers as they traveled from one funeral site to another. There were upbeat moments accompanied by laughter and horseplay—and always lots of spontaneous singing. By the end of the journey, it's safe to say that there were few onboard who didn't know at least one stanza of the black church hymn "We've Come This Far by Faith." All during the trip, caravan passengers sang spirit-lifting songs that reinforced a message of hope that some way, somehow, everything was going to be all right.

Audience participation on the bus trip didn't end with song. As a means of coping, the passengers—one by one—got out of their seats and shared their fondest memories of the players who died. These testimonial-style presentations helped everyone on the bus to learn more about the human side of these deceased athletes.

Melancholy moments were to be expected. Every time the bus would get within forty to forty-five minutes of arriving at the next funeral stop, the mood would change dramatically. Bus riders went from being jovial to being in mourning. At those times, silence gripped the atmosphere. With the exception of some quiet chatter here and there, the only sound was the barely audible hum of the engine as the bus motored down the highway. This aura of quietness remained when passengers boarded the bus after attending a homegoing. The silence would last for as long as an hour or two. At times, the stillness was so obvious that you could hear a mosquito breathe.

These extremes in shifting emotions played out time after time over the course of this trip. "At one point, you felt terribly sad," said Bundy. "But then you felt a closeness, a togetherness, a love for each other; and you felt how *everybody* was holding up everybody else."

Larry Carter's smooth skills with the bus microphone helped his fellow passengers deal with their respective emotional roller coasters. His presence was sorely needed to break those long stretches of silence while establishing a lighter mood in the process. In his tenor voice reminiscent of a jazz deejay, L.C. would ask, *"What's happenin' and thangs?"*

That question always seemed to get everybody's attention. From that point on, everybody on that bus became prime targets for his comical attacks, which ran the gamut from personal clothing styles to the ugly faces people make after they wake up from sleeping. In many ways, Larry Carter had far deeper ties with the players than others on the caravan. He was a three-year starter for the Herd at tight end whose eligibility expired after the 1969 season. Back then, athletes had three years of varsity eligibility because freshmen were not allowed to play varsity. The year of the crash, LC was finishing up his last two semesters prior to graduating and earning an officer's commission in the US Army.

The caravan maintained a hectic schedule during its first full day. The group made two of its four homegoing stops, beginning with the services in Bluefield and ending with a wake in Atlanta on Friday night.

Those in attendance at Blevins's funeral represented a balanced racial cross-section of mourners who filled the pews to near capacity. Blevins, a revered three-sport star, was one of a handful of black Catholics in Bluefield at that time. While his church family was overwhelmingly white, Blev's kinship ties and other social connections were rooted in the black community.

"Paulette (Dodson) Scott, a junior in '70, found herself coming to grips with reality as she sat silently with her peers in the sanctuary. "The first funeral was the hardest because it was the first," said Paulette, a cousin of Bill and Angela Dodson. "I can't say that things got any better as we went to the other funerals. By the time we had gone to three services, you just learned to deal with it and you adjusted as best you could."

*   *   *

The long ride from Bluefield resulted in a late arrival in Atlanta, sometime around eleven thirty at night. It was past the funeral home's business hours, but arrangements to conduct a service there had been made earlier.

The funeral home opened its doors for the Marshall delegation to have a memorial service for Larry "The Governor" Brown that lasted about forty minutes. Logistics dictated that a wake would be held on Friday night. Brown's funeral was set for Saturday, the same day the caravan was due to be in Alabama for the funeral of the four Tuscaloosa athletes.

Even though the visitors from West Virginia did not stay at the funeral home for very long, they were able to spend some quality time with Brown's family. "We didn't spend much time there, but you still got the sense that us being there was very important to Larry's family," Bundy said. "We came away feeling like we were able to help in some way or another."

*   *   *

Huntington, West Virginia: A crowd of less than 1,000 people show up at Fairfield Stadium one week after the plane crash for a memorial service to honor the victims. The one-thirty starting time was purposely set to coincide with the kickoff time for the canceled Marshall-Ohio University game that would have been played in Athens, Ohio, that day.

The low attendance was hardly surprising. There were still funerals to attend. Many of those connected with the school were out of town that weekend for that reason.

A wreath was placed at midfield and the Reverend Robert Scott of the MU Campus Christian Center led everyone in prayer. Reverend Scott was also the Thundering Herd's team chaplain. Around the country, there were similar tributes given in recognition of the Marshall team at other college football games that were played that day.

The memorial service at Fairfield Stadium wasn't part of the caravan. But it did take place the same weekend the caravan made its various funeral stops.

*   *   *

Reggie Oliver left home in August of '70 to attend college with some close friends. It was Oliver's freshman year, and he couldn't wait to get to Marshall University to help his friends in their agreed-upon mission to help the Thundering Herd become a college football power. He had no clue that less than four months after leaving, he'd return to Tuscaloosa,

Alabama, to pay his final respects to four guys who grew up together and played ball together at the same high school and at the same college.

Four closed caskets were positioned side by side at the front of the auditorium at Druid High School. A portrait sat on top of each fallen player's casket. The joint funeral for Larry Sanders, Joe Hood, Robert VanHorn, and Freddy Wilson attracted a standing-room-only crowd of more than 2,500. Former teammates from high school and college served as pallbearers. The Druid choir stirred souls and touched hearts when they sang "The Lord Is My Shepherd" and "Unto Thee O Lord."

Oliver was greeted by an endless number of well-wishers after he entered the auditorium prior to the start of the service. Just as he was about to get to the orchestra pit area where the caskets were located, a woman sitting in the second row near the aisle tugged at his sleeve coat and pulled him by the arm. Oliver sensed from the pulling motion that this woman wanted him to bend down low enough where she could talk to him without being overheard. Oliver declined to identify the woman but acknowledged that she was the mother of one of the players who died.

"As I came down the aisle, different people kept asking me what had happened, and after a while, I got tunnel vision," Oliver said. "I was going to touch each casket. That's what I wanted to do. I leaned down and she asked me a question (pointing to one of the caskets): 'All I want to know is—is that my son in there?'

"As for how I answered the question, I'll keep that between the mother and me," he said. "Her question was legitimate. It was a very emotional time for her and for me. I took my seat, and, from that point on, I was in Never Never Land. I don't recall any of the proceedings from the service."

Oliver's brief talk with that mother was not the last time he heard from that family on that day. After the service, that mother's husband (father of one of the deceased) gave Oliver a phone call. It wasn't what he expected, and it only added to his bereavement. As hurtful as it was, he understood the rationale and had no problem complying with the husband's request: "I know you guys (Reggie and his son) were close," the husband and father said. "But my wife is really having a hard time right now. So, it would be best if you don't come over to the house. She's used to seeing the both of you together all the time. When she sees you, she automatically thinks of him. She's in so much pain because he's gone. I hope you understand."

Ed Carter didn't ride the bus but traveled to Alabama by car with some Marshall basketball players. He remembers an incredibly gut-wrenching moment. During the service, a grieving parent of one of the players cried out in anguish. "Why did my son have to die in that crash? Why were the others not on that plane?"

That's not something you'd expect to hear at a funeral. All-consuming grief can cause people to make statements they wouldn't otherwise make. Ed recognized that the parent's reference to "the others" included him and those players who did not travel to East Carolina. "I could tell it was directed at me, even though nobody said anything to me specifically," Ed said. "It was emotional and very understandable. I had no reaction. I did not say anything back."

A sizeable portion of the folks who attended the joint funeral made their way to the cemetery. At least 1,000 people showed up at Cedar Oak Memorial Park. The four players were interred in burial plots located right next to each other.

Before the preachers finished speaking their final words at the gravesites, Larry Sanders's girlfriend, Macie Lugo, slipped away from the huge crowd. Murrial Jarrett, Macie's best friend at Marshall, accompanied her. Given the highly charged emotional atmosphere of the day, it was time to get some solitude, if only for a few moments. The two walked until they were about fifty yards away from the crowd.

Murrial couldn't understand what was going on with Macie, who had said very little and appeared to be completely detached from her surroundings. Murrial stood directly in front of Macie, looked at her face to face, and repeatedly expressed her concerns. "Talk to me, Macie. What are you feeling? Why aren't you crying? Why aren't you showing any emotion? Please don't keep this bottled up inside you."

Macie said nothing.

Murrial took Macie by the hand. The two walked away in silence and got in a car to return to the place they were staying for the weekend.

"My biggest concern about Macie was that she never showed any emotion," said Murrial, who was in her senior year. "She took on that Jackie Kennedy kind of persona. She was the stoic, dignified, grieving girlfriend. At the cemetery, I tried to get her to let her emotions out. But by then, she was already in that quiet, stoic mode. It was easy to see that this (death of Larry Sanders) was the hurt of her life. It was painful. The hurt ran very deep to her inner being. I don't think she ever got over it."

Al Evans and several of his Marshall schoolmates endured some hardships on the trip to Tuscaloosa, but difficulties did not deter them from reaching their destination. Evans developed a deep and lasting bond with Freddy Wilson, who frequently went home with him on weekends during the summer months.

Evans and a second carload of Marshall students took off for Alabama to attend the services, and he rode in Freddy's car. The twelve-hour trip took much longer than it was supposed to. Freddy's '62 Ford Falcon broke down on the way, and it didn't help that no one among the traveling crew could read a road map correctly. They kept getting lost, which added a few more hours to their already lengthy trek through the South.

Since only one of the cars was now operable, the passengers and luggage from Freddy's Ford were stuffed into a second vehicle, so now there were seven passengers riding around in cramped quarters like sardines packed in a can. Once they arrived in Tuscaloosa, they stopped at an apartment complex to verify where they would stay while in town. They were not part of the caravan, so they were responsible for making their own overnight sleeping arrangements.

While they were inside one of the apartments in the complex, thieves apparently labeled the car as an easy mark because of the out-of-state license plate. They broke in the car and stole every piece of luggage. The local Jaycees made good of a bad situation and provided some funds to purchase apparel so that Evans and the others had clothes to wear to the funeral.

"It wasn't a very comfortable ride," Evans recalled. "At that point, nobody really complained. We just did what we had to do. Your mind wasn't on anything you might have to deal with. It was more about sorting through your own emotions (about the crash). Freddy was a big, friendly, good-natured guy. You knew he would always have your back."

The tragic deaths of the four athletes caused the community to wonder why they chose to travel so far from home to go to college. There was the pervasive sentiment among the folks in "T-town" that Sanders, Hood, VanHorn, and Wilson should never have had to leave the state to play prime-time college football in the first place.

Skin color—not skill—was the issue. In the late '60s, white colleges in the South would not recruit blacks. In Alabama, it was accepted as fact among the coaches that white college football fans were not ready to embrace black athletes. For blacks who wanted to play at a predominantly white school, the only options were to go north or to the West Coast.

It is generally believed that the racial complexion of college football changed drastically in '70 when the integrated University of Southern California crushed an all-white University of Alabama team in a nationally televised game. Sam "Bam" Cunningham, a black fullback, bulled his way for 135 yards and two touchdowns in a decisive 42-21 victory. In the years to follow, Southern white schools began to tap into the talent pool that had been the exclusive domain of the historically black colleges. 'Bama signed its first black player—Wilbur Jackson—months before the start of the '70 season. Wilbur, however, was reduced to being a spectator in his first year of college. NCAA rules prohibited freshmen from playing varsity in those days.

The city of Tuscaloosa welcomed the Marshall contingent with open arms and Stillman College eagerly accepted its role as host. Stillman, a predominantly black school, served a full-course breakfast buffet and made its dorm rooms available for sleeping quarters. The hospitality didn't stop there. After the funeral, some Stillman students hosted a get-together for the Marshall group that night.

In some people's minds, going out to party just hours after coming from a funeral is grossly inappropriate. That's not the case when it comes to black culture. "To me, it was like a goal the Stillman students had was to help ease the pain we were going through," said Lawson Brooks, a Marshall freshman at the time of the tragedy. "As we sat around and talked, we felt like the guys would want us to go on. They wouldn't want us to dwell on the sadness of it all. It was a strange kind of feeling. I saw the party more as an outgrowth of their love for us. The students at Stillman really reached out to us."

*   *   *

Of all the caravan stops, Greenwood, South Carolina, was clearly the most rural. No city skyline. No expressway. No streetlight on every corner. No signs of the hustle and bustle associated with places like Columbia and Charleston, the two biggest cities in the state. Greenwood is located in the northwest section of South Carolina, and is not that far from the Georgia border.

To get to the church where Willie Bluford's funeral was held, the bus traveled down a long country road surrounded by what looked like a corn field. Eventually the bus came to a clearing and pulled up to the front entrance of a small building that was painted in a milky-white color. A cemetery was located on church grounds.

Inside, there was not a lot of pew space. At best, this church wasn't built to accommodate more than sixty people, and the members of the caravan occupied nearly every seat. With Bluford's family and friends in attendance, plus the people from Marshall, folks were lined up along the walls and there may have been even more people standing outside the front door. The space was tight, practically elbow-to-elbow.

Even though this was late November, this was still the Deep South where steamy temperatures are the norm, even at that time of year. There was no air conditioning, no ceiling fan, and no floor fan. The sole source of relief: those trusty hand-held fans that worked overtime on that day.

The rustic setting in Greenwood was reminiscent of the past, a time in which previous generations of black people made their livelihood off the land as farmers or sharecroppers.

After Bluford's homegoing on Sunday, a weary troupe of travelers headed home to Marshall late that afternoon and arrived back on campus some time after midnight. The job of saying farewell was completed, and it was good to be back in familiar surroundings. This group shared so many highs and lows during this trip. And they harvested a lifetime's worth of memories that we now view as history.

Some went to class on Monday. Others slept for most of the day, knowing they would be leaving again in a few days to go on Thanksgiving break. More time to unwind, more time to reflect.

"Coming back," Brooks explained, "everyone was pretty much drained. But, we all came back with a greater sense, not only for the guys who died, but better feelings for each other. By going on this trip, it made me appreciate my life a lot more. It made me want to accomplish certain things, knowing that life is not promised, that it can all be gone in a moment."

For Angela Dodson, the caravan journey provided her with a viable means to deal with a great loss. "During that whole time, you kept thinking that this just couldn't be real," she said. "That trip gave all of us a way to honor the memory of those players in a way that took away that sense of helplessness. The act of going to all those funerals performed that function of doing something concrete, rather than sitting around on campus and hearing about everything later on."

*   *   *

Paying homage to the deceased black football players did not stop when the caravan returned to campus. The Southern sojourn proved to be the launching pad for the Soul Searchers of First Baptist in Huntington. The group initially started out as a church fellowship for college students, and Scottie Reese was the first president. After the crash, however, the fellowship group was transformed into a gospel ensemble that also performed drama on stage.

The production was divided into two segments. The first portion of the program featured an improvised version of the Broadway musical *Purlie*. The second half consisted of a combination of poetry, dance, singing, and prayer. These additions enhanced the Soul Searchers' presentation as they paid tribute to their dearly departed schoolmates.

"This became our way of telling our story," said Paulette Scott, a Soul Searchers dancer. "We also got to experience new things which gave us hope. I learned that there is a future, and even though traumatic things occur, you have to keep moving forward. As you see and experience more positive things, you understand that there is so much more to see and do."

The Soul Searchers put together two tours in the months following the tragedy. They went on their inaugural tour during spring break of '71, which included visits to Richmond, Virginia, and four northern cities: New York, Philadelphia, Boston, and Springfield (Massachusetts). During their time in the New England region, the Soul Searchers toured Harvard University and Massachusetts Institute of Technology,

That summer, the group embarked on a Reconciliation Tour that played in four Southern cities. The tour kicked off with dates in Bluefield, West Virginia, and Jacksonville, Florida, and it ended with stops in two Texas cities: Dallas and Waco. In Bundy's mind, these tours were a natural continuation of the Homegoing Caravan.

Reconciliation was the theme for the Southern tour. Aside from honoring the crash victims through prayer, song, poetry, dance, and dramatic productions, this tour had an added purpose: to demonstrate the need for blacks and whites to peacefully coexist. In the late '60s/early '70s, racial tensions still plagued many parts of the country. It was the group's desire that through their performances, their message of unity among the races would come through loud and clear.

"Everybody knows how athletics brings people from all types of backgrounds together," said Bundy, who performed with the forty-member tour group. "But we also saw how the tragedy brought people even closer together."

The highlight of the Southern tour was the performance at Paul Quinn College, headquartered in Waco at that time (relocated to Dallas in 1990). Waco is Scottie's hometown and it's also his final resting place. Most Soul Searchers members developed a strong connection with Scottie, which explains why they shed tears of sorrow mixed with tears of joy in honoring his memory.

Soul Searchers drummer Bill Redd remembers Waco as being the most emotional stop on the tour. "Scottie's father (Chester) was humbled to see us," Redd said. "He was glad to know that his son was very active with us. It was a humbling experience for him and for the group. Scottie was a young man, twenty years old, whose life was snatched away. It was earth-shaking, devastating."

The impact of the plane crash was both personal and collective for the people who lived through it. They are forever connected by this singular event. For Marshall's black students, a tangible and lasting bond was forged, and it's as strong today as it was in the days and months following the disaster.

Chapter Six

They Were Spared

"The Lord saved me to serve Him. He had his hand on my life, and He separated me from my team for that very purpose."

Dr. Ed Carter
Former MU offensive lineman

The story of the Marshall plane crash has many angles. So many, that it would be virtually impossible for any one media source to cover every single aspect. I don't know every detail about every angle. What I do know is this: Ed Carter, Felix Jordan, and Dickie Carter (no relation to Ed) are the missing pieces. Without their input, the story is incomplete.

Ed Carter is thoroughly convinced that divine intervention saved his life. Twelve days *before* the crash, he got a long-distance phone call one afternoon after practice. It was his mother calling from Wichita Falls, Texas. She broke the news that Ed's father had died, and that Ed was to leave school and come home for the funeral. During the course of that conversation, Sarah Word emphatically told her son that he should *not go* to East Carolina. She explained that the plane would crash and that there would be *no survivors*. Ed, a starter at offensive tackle, played in a home game later that week, and then left town for Texas on the Monday prior to the East Carolina road trip.

Ed was stunned and puzzled by what his mother told him.

How could Mom know this and be so sure about it actually happening? he thought. *And how could she know about a plane trip that I didn't even know about? We always traveled by bus for away games.*

During the week before going home for his father's funeral, Ed never mentioned the conversation he had with his mom to anyone. In his mind, the idea was simply too farfetched to take seriously. "I didn't believe there would be a plane crash," he said.

Ed had sufficient time to make it back to West Virginia to rejoin the team for its upcoming game. He had a roundtrip plane ticket, so he could have returned in time to get in two days of practice. In the meantime, Sarah kept insisting that Ed remain in Wichita Falls for a few more days. He wanted to get back to playing football, but eventually his mother was able to change his mind.

"Once I got back to Texas, Mom never mentioned anything about a plane crash," he said. "All she kept saying was how I needed to stay and help console my younger brothers. Every time she told me she didn't want me to go, she'd start crying. I didn't like seeing her cry, so I decided to stay home just to satisfy her."

Sarah's words proved to be prophetic. The night of the crash, Ed was on the phone with a friend when he heard the radio news bulletin about the tragedy in far-away West Virginia. "I was just stunned," he recalled, "everything happened so quickly."

The next day, Ed read about the disaster in the local paper, which erroneously listed him as one of the casualties. "It was like reading my own obituary," he said. On that night and over the next few days, the phone never stopped ringing. Concerned friends and neighbors called to express their condolences. Ed answered some of the calls, which provided some much-needed relief for those who assumed that he was with the Marshall team.

"In later discussions, my mom said that it was not a premonition when she told me about what would happen," Ed said. "She made it clear that God gave her that revelation as we talked. After the crash, it didn't take much to persuade me to ride the bus back to West Virginia."

During the twenty-eight-hour bus ride back to Huntington, Ed could not escape the constant visual reminders of the tragedy. At every bus station, it seemed, every paper in the news racks featured front-page stories about the crash. The huge headlines in bold-faced type verified a chilling fact. Most of Ed's teammates died in that crash, but for some reason that was yet to be discovered, his life had been spared.

Once Ed returned to West Virginia, he noticed a stark difference from what life was like before the tragedy and afterward. The somber mood of a city and campus in mourning was clearly evident. "It was like a ghost town almost," he said. "Everybody was down and depressed and discouraged. It was so disheartening."

By the start of the week following the crash, a lot of people knew that Ed Carter was not on the plane. The fact that his life had been spared, however, was not common knowledge to everyone. Ed discovered this after having a bizarre encounter with a schoolmate not long after he returned from Texas. Ida Franklin, a black coed at Marshall, saw Ed and immediately did an about-face. She started walking so swiftly in the opposite direction that it seemed like she was getting ready to run. "Ida looked at me as if she had seen a ghost," Ed recalled. "I had to run to catch up with her. She had a hard time believing I was still alive. I explained what had happened and that helped her to calm down."

The November tragedy proved to be Ed's avenue for change in his personal life. Two months before his college graduation in 1974, he gave his life to Christ. That same year, he answered God's call to preach and he started Death Unto Life Ministries, headquartered in Chattanooga, Tennessee. The foundation for Ed's ministry is rooted in his escape from the fatal plane crash. During its thirty-seven years of existence, Death Unto Life Ministries has touched hundreds of thousands in the United States and around the world.

"The Lord saved me to serve Him," Ed explained. "He had his hand on my life and He separated me from my team for that very purpose. For all these years, I've been an unofficial ambassador for Marshall University. Everywhere I go, I tell people about how He saved me from the plane crash, saved my soul, and placed me in ministry. I passed from death unto life when I trusted Christ to be my Savior. I've been given a variety of opportunities to reach people that I never would have reached, had it not been for the testimony that God has given me."

> *Verily, verily, I say unto you, He that heareth my word, and believeth on Him that sent me, hath everlasting life, and shall not come into condemnation; but is passed from death unto life.*

> *John 5:24*
> *(King James Version of the Bible)*

At speaking engagements, Ed Carter frequently displays a laminated copy of the story from his hometown newspaper that named him as one of the seventy-five passengers who were killed. That news article serves as a compelling visual tool. It helps Ed to effectively deliver his message about God's intervention in rescuing him from a horrific plane crash.

One of the most touching moments in Ed Carter's ministry occurred ten years after he started Death Unto Life. On this occasion, he was one of the featured speakers at a revival held in Proctorville, Ohio, a small town located less than three miles across the bridge from Huntington.

Whenever Ed preaches in the Huntington area, he always encourages former teammates and schoolmates to attend the services. Some have declined Ed's invitations, but there were others who came as a show of respect. Nate Ruffin brought his family to one of the revival services that week. Nate, who played three varsity seasons (1969–1971), had heard Ed preach on many other occasions.

On this night, things would be different. As Ed finished his sermon, a teary-eyed Nate approached the altar and gave his life to Christ.

Ed and Nate were both starters on Marshall's varsity in '70. They missed the East Carolina road trip, but for different reasons. Ruffin was not on the plane because of a season-ending injury.

Ruffin's desire to get saved after hearing his ex-teammate preach provides one more bit of irony to the Marshall football saga. Nate and Ed both lost teammates in a terrible calamity, and both were on hand to help a struggling football program get back on its feet. Ed has a ministry today, all because he heeded a prophetic warning from his mother.

It took around fourteen years or so *after the crash* for Ruffin's conversion to take place. There's no doubt that Ed's sermon was the vehicle the Lord used to convince Ed's former teammate that it was time for him to surrender his life to Christ.

That same night, Ruffin requested a private consultation with Ed in one of the pastor's offices at the church. Even though he was a successful business executive and prominent figure with the local chamber of commerce and the Jaycees, Ruffin was not satisfied with his life. "Nate was in tears as he talked about some of his accomplishments," Ed said. "He told me that in spite of all that he had done, he felt like he had nothing."

The next night of the revival, Ruffin was there. The call from the pulpit exhorted everyone in the pews to take part in "popcorn testimony." This is where people—as they are moved by the Holy Spirit—get up out of their seats and tell what the Lord has done in their lives. The spontaneity of these testimonies is reminiscent of what you see when watching a bag of popcorn being prepared in a microwave oven.

Ruffin did not hesitate to speak. He literally jumped out of his seat to share his story. "I was surprised," Ed admits. "Nate had just gotten saved one night earlier, so he really didn't know anything about giving a testimony."

It didn't matter. Ruffin spoke from his heart, and everybody in the audience knew it. He acknowledged that restoration for everyone is always available through God. Years earlier, Ruffin assumed an active role in helping to resurrect Marshall's football program. And now, thanks to some soul-stirring words from a preacher who was also a friend, Ruffin began to experience restoration on a personal level. What Ruffin said that night is still fresh in Ed's mind.

"I can't hold it no longer," Ruffin confessed to the congregation. "I've been running from the Lord for all these years, and I've heard Ed preach over here and over there. But last night, God tackled me, so I'm not running away any more."

Ruffin, who was later ordained as a deacon, served in a variety of capacities as an avid Marshall supporter. When the Herd played in its first Division I-AA national championship game in '87, he wasn't interested in watching it on television like most of the Marshall faithful. He wanted to be there in person. Getting there by air was out of the question because all flights were already booked. That's when he decided to hitchhike 1,844 miles from Huntington to Pocatello, Idaho, to attend that game.

Because of the time factor, driving his own car or traveling by bus or train was not a reasonable solution for Nate. By car, it would take at least two days of nonstop driving. But that would work *only* if there were enough passengers on hand to take turns driving, which would allow enough time for every driver to get sufficient rest. The schedules for buses and trains included so many stopovers that the trip would take even longer than it would by car.

I can't say why Nate chose to hitchhike, but I can offer an opinion based on our relationship as former teammates. Nate had an infectious personality. He had an inbred ability to connect with people from all walks of life. Nate Ruffin was the kind of guy who never met a stranger. However, I do believe there was one compelling reason that fueled Nate's desire to go to Idaho. When Marshall's football freshmen finished the season undefeated in '68, all of us on that team shared a collective vision. We were determined that by our senior year, Marshall would win a MAC championship and play in the Tangerine Bowl in Florida. We fell short of achieving our goal. But nineteen years later, *Marshall was playing for a national championship—in football.* This was the culmination of a vision that finally did come to pass. And the only way to fully bask in that experience was to physically be there in the stands, watching all the action as it unfolded.

Nate was heavily involved with several MU presidential search committees and was a member of the school's Alumni Board of Directors. In addition to his contributions as an athletics booster and recruiter, he was also active in Black Alumni of Marshall University. The Alumni Lounge in the Erickson Alumni Center on campus is named for Ruffin. Black Alumni secured the naming rights with a $100,000 pledge.

Ruffin died of leukemia in 2001 and is buried at the memorial site for the '70 team at Spring Hill Cemetery located on Huntington's south side. A year prior to his passing away, Nate read an open letter to his departed teammates that aired on the ABC network during halftime of the 2000 MAC title game between Marshall and Western Michigan. It was the thirtieth anniversary of the crash. (The open letter can be viewed on the Internet on You Tube.)

"For awhile, I wished I was with you guys," Nate said in his letter. "But I realize now, many years later, that I was left here to keep your memory alive."

*   *   *

Felix Jordan, the starting free safety, missed the trip because of a last-minute change of plans. On the day the team left town, Felix had settled into his seat on the bus that would take the team to the airport. But just prior to departure, one of the coaches asked him to give up his seat to one of the MU athletic boosters, who were helping to pay for the cost of the flight. That wasn't the only reason Felix was left behind. Somebody on the coaching staff decided it would be better for Felix to stay home. Sitting out the ECU game would give him an additional week to heal and be ready for the season finale against Ohio University. Due to the lateness of the passenger switch, Felix's equipment made it to East Carolina, but he didn't.

Known as "X-Ray," Felix was not healthy enough to play that weekend. He suffered a severe ankle injury in the homecoming game against Western

Michigan. It's unlikely that he would have seen any action against East Carolina anyway. "I remember the play when I was injured," Felix told me. "It happened when I came up to tackle Roger Lawson (Western Michigan running back). *That play* probably saved my life."

Felix, who lives in Blue Ash, Ohio, admits that thoughts of the crash cross his mind every day. Over the years, he's had dreams and flashbacks. At times, he's found himself talking to deceased teammates.

Felix spoke candidly to the *Cincinnati Enquirer* newspaper around Christmas 2006 about his recollections of 1970. (The article in its entirety appears in the appendix.)

The night of the crash, Felix was hanging out with friends at the Student Union. Moments after hearing the news, he and several MU athletes hopped in a car and sped to the airport.

When they arrived at the site, all they could do was stand and watch, frozen by the cold and shock. The whole side of the mountain was consumed by a raging fire caused by the explosion from the crash. Felix returned to the scene the next day. There were no more flames, but the hillside was still smoldering. He desperately wanted to help identify his teammates, but emotionally he just wasn't up to the task.

Felix didn't know what to make of everything that had happened. Football players are supposed to the poster boys for toughness and grit, the ultimate examples of machismo. Football players aren't supposed to show emotions that might indicate even the slightest hint of weakness of any kind. Felix wasn't concerned about examples and what football players were supposed to be like as far as their inner feelings. All he knew was that most of the people who were the closest to him at Marshall—his teammates—were gone in the blink of an eye. They were like family. The sudden loss was such a jolt, such a shock, so unbelievable, so overwhelming. Felix couldn't hold back the tears.

Even to this day, Felix wonders why he's still here.

*   *   *

Dickie Carter played in 1970 but did not finish his senior season. He quit the team after the second game because of a dispute with Coach Tolley, so he was not on the plane. A punishing fullback at five feet, nine inches and 225 pounds, Dickie was nicknamed "Sled Dog" because of his ability to drag tacklers. For unknown reasons, he was never approached about participating in any media projects related to Marshall's football program.

For all intents and purposes, he's *persona non grata*.

It's as if he never existed.

That's so strange. Dickie was a key factor for the Thundering Herd for most of his college career. As a sophomore, he was Marshall's top kickoff-return specialist—he averaged 24.9 yards per return in '68. Dickie played a pivotal role in the team's late-season turnaround when the Herd won three of its last four games in '69. Over the final half of that season, he averaged nearly 4.5 yards per carry and emerged as a dependable receiver. Everything was in place for Dickie to excel in his final college season.

The Herd added the wishbone to its offensive arsenal, which featured Dickie, Art Harris, and Joe Hood as backfield mates. With those three on the field at the same time, Marshall had the right ingredients for a dynamite ground game. Each back had a different style, but all were equally effective. Opponents would have had a tough time slowing down that threesome. Here's what Coach Tolley said about Dickie in the Herd's football media guide for '70: "Dickie should really help us this year. He's been running better than ever and we're expecting great things of him this fall."

Given that brief snapshot of Dickie's college career, there's no debate about his relevance to the '70 team.

In terms of media coverage, the only link between Dickie and the Thundering Herd comes in *Ashes to Glory*, a documentary about the plane crash and the subsequent restoration of Marshall University football. A quickie reference to Dickie lasts all of one millisecond.

There's a segment in *Ashes to Glory* where Nate Ruffin talks about his whereabouts on the night of the crash. He was watching a movie at one of the downtown theaters. Before the movie ended, one of the theater managers interrupted the viewing to tell the audience about a crash at Tri-State Airport.

Ruffin bolted from his seat and went outside, hoping to find a way to get to the scene. He looked around and immediately spotted Dickie, who just happened to be driving by the theater on his way back to campus. When they saw one another, there wasn't much of a need for conversation. Ruffin got in Dickie's car, and they were on their way to the airport. As Nate speaks about seeing Dickie Carter, a picture of Dickie appears briefly, but there's no mention of him in the documentary after that.

"If you blink, you'll miss it," Dickie said. "As far as I'm concerned, it doesn't matter if somebody was injured and wasn't on the plane, or if they quit the team. You always remember your teammates. I've heard through others that people felt like I betrayed the team. If you had seen me that night, you would never have known that I had quit playing. My sense of loss was just as much as Nate's, or anybody else's, maybe more. I really admired the players. They were the future for Marshall."

The great things Tolley expected of Sled Dog never materialized. By the third or fourth week of the season, Dickie was gone, and it wasn't because of an injury. What turned out to be Dickie's final college game is one that he would just as soon forget. Marshall suffered a 52-3 beat-down whipping at the hands of the University of Toledo. And it was as bad as the final score indicated.

In and of itself, losing to Toledo was a not a disgrace. The Rockets, three-time Tangerine Bowl champions, were a genuine powerhouse during that era. They put together a thirty-five-game win streak from 1969 to 1971, which is No. 2 in the NCAA record books behind record holder Oklahoma, which won forty-seven games in a row from 1953 to 1957.

In Dickie's mind, Coach Tolley had unfairly singled him out as being one of the prime reasons why Marshall took such a whipping. When practice resumed, Dickie knew he would be expected to run lots and lots of sprints. This was not out of the ordinary. Tolley had a reputation for conducting boot-camp-style practices.

Ruffin described what practices were like under Tolley in the book *The Marshall Story*, which takes a chronological look at the football program from the late '60s through 2005. "We found ourselves literally being beat to death on the practice field. We called Tolley the 'Dog Man.' We said the man was fair; he treated everybody like dogs."

Although it was not his intention, Dickie came to a decision about his football future during a practice session after the Toledo blow-out loss. "He (Tolley) would have everybody come together and would call out different players' names, then make them run sprints. Run, run, run; run until you pass out," Dickie said.

"During a practice the week after the Toledo game, Coach Tolley asked me if I owed him something (wind sprints). I didn't use any curse words, but I took my helmet off and told him he could take my helmet and shove it. That's when I walked off the field. I quit right then. It wasn't just me who had a bad game, it was all of us. I felt like I was being picked on. I thank God that I made that choice."

Dickie says some of the players and assistant coaches approached him about reconsidering. Sled Dog hoped that Coach Tolley would personally contact him about coming back. For whatever reason, they never talked. There would be no comeback.

On that cold and drizzly Saturday night of November 14, Dickie visited some friends off campus. He was looking forward to celebrating his twenty-second birthday on Monday. While watching television, he read the news flash as it streamed across the bottom of the screen. The Marshall plane had crashed, but there was no word yet about the condition of the passengers. A follow-up report later confirmed that everyone onboard had perished. As the news coverage continued, a picture of Marshall's starting backfield was shown, and Dickie was in that picture. He learned later that folks in his hometown of Man, West Virginia, saw that same picture on a local newscast, so they were inclined to believe that Sled Dog had died. The only person in Dickie's family who knew about him leaving the team was one of his brothers.

Not sure what he should do next, Dickie left his friend's house and drove back to campus. Passing through downtown, Dickie saw Nate, and they went to the airport. When they arrived at the crash area, they could only get so close. The intensity of the heat caused by the burning jet fuel when the plane crashed was so great, it could be felt from the highway, which was less than a half-mile away.

"Everybody stood around crying and consoling each other for a long time, maybe for an hour or two," Dickie said. "This didn't seem real. All my friends; all my teammates; gone. This just couldn't be happening. It was more like a dream."

The remainder of that night was an exercise in restless wandering. Dickie left the crash scene and called home, but the phone lines were busy and he couldn't get through. He didn't want to return to campus; and he didn't want to risk an accident in driving home to Man, a two-hour drive from school. So he remained in Huntington, spent the night in his car, and kept driving around with no particular destination in mind. He'd stop on occasion and take a short nap. It wasn't until after sunrise on Sunday morning that Dickie returned to campus. He called home again. This time, he was able to talk to somebody . . . *finally*.

"I'm told that there were a lot of phone calls at the house that night," he said. "A lot of my friends showed up at the house crying and expressing their sorrow. Even though my mother and I had not talked before that Sunday morning, she said that she *just knew* I was still alive. Mom was a praying woman. She felt that if something had happened to me, God would have told her."

Dickie was so shaken by the disaster that he purposely avoided attending any funerals or memorial services. The days following the tragedy were painful and difficult for everyone. To make matters worse, Dickie was convinced that news reporters tried to bait him into making negative statements about Tolley. To this day, the insinuation that Dickie wished Tolley harm still saddens him.

"The way they asked questions was very cold and non-caring," he said. "They asked me how I felt about Tolley. I told them I didn't wish for him to be dead, I wish he was still alive. Him being dead didn't change the fact that we didn't get along."

Things were never the same for Dickie. He left school at the end of that semester and eventually moved north.

"I wanted to go (and pay my respects), but it tore me up so badly, I just couldn't go," he said. "Everybody was in mourning. You kept expecting to see the guys sitting around in the dorms—talking, joking, playing cards. In one of my classes, the professor started calling roll, and when the names of players who had died were called, people started crying, and class was dismissed for that day. The same thing happened in some of my other classes too. After a while, I decided against coming back to school. I couldn't go back. My mind wasn't right."

Even though several decades have passed since the crash, Dickie recalls in striking detail the mood of the Marshall players in the days leading up to the crash. He remembers how different things were during that week compared to other times when the team made preparations to go on the road. As usual, the players sat around the dorm lobby, but there was an eerie quietness to the point where the atmosphere was resoundingly somber. There was no laughter or joking around. No music, no card games, no ladies. Observing all this caused Dickie to question Dave DeBord, an offensive lineman.

"Why all the sad faces?" Dickie asked.

"If I could just make it back from this trip, I'll be very happy," said DeBord.

"Dave, it's going to be all right."

DeBord didn't respond verbally. His body language, though, indicated that he wasn't totally buying into Dickie's attempts to reassure him. To Dickie, it seemed like the whole team had a collective mind-set that something bad was going to happen—as if it was a foregone conclusion. That week, several Marshall players gave a lot of their personal possessions to friends, girlfriends, and relatives.

Not everybody on the team was all that eager to travel by air. Tight end Freddy Wilson made it known that if it was up to him, he would ride the truck to East Carolina with John Hagan, the equipment manager. Hagan decided not to go to East Carolina by plane. According to Dickie, Hagan told folks that a black bird flew through a window in his house on Friday the 13th, which is considered a sign of bad luck. So instead of flying, Hagan drove.

Up until 1999, Dickie, now a retired postal worker who lives in Alexandria, Virginia, had recurring dreams about the plane going down with him in it.

The dream would always end with Dickie standing in the midst of the wreckage while he watched the plane and its contents go up in flames. The visions were so disturbing that he had trouble going to sleep most of the time. Not only that, but Dickie made a habit of sleeping with the lights on, and he started drinking—a lot.

"That was the lowest point in my life," he said. "I was never suicidal, and I never became an alcoholic. But I've had thoughts that maybe I was supposed to be with them (on the plane). Sometimes I get real emotional when I think about it. There are times when I feel like I let my teammates down because I wasn't there."

Through the years, Dickie has wrestled with the fact that his life was spared. On many occasions, he has approached several ministers in an effort to gain some kind of insight on why he's still here. He felt compelled to ask the same question of every minister he talked to. Every time he asked, he would always get the same answer, but the answer would come from a different minister. Here's how the exchange would go.

"Would the Lord take a lot of lives just to save a few?" Dickie would inquire.

"Don't question God," the ministers advised. "He does everything for a reason. Everything He does is for a purpose."

Dickie has never felt completely comfortable about coming back to Marshall. His one and only visit came in '84, the inaugural year for the school's sports hall of fame induction ceremonies. He got an invitation in the mail to attend HOF weekend but didn't respond right away. It took more than a week for him to come to a decision. And even then, had it not been for some persistent nudging from his wife, Harriett, and his sister Shirley Rankin, he would've stayed home. It's anyone's guess as to whether or not Dickie will ever return to the Marshall campus again. "My wife and sister had to convince me," he confessed. "I really didn't know if I would be accepted or not. I got the impression that some of the people there might still hold it against me because I quit the team."

It wouldn't take long for Dickie to find out if his apprehension was justified. Not long after he and his wife arrived at the induction dinner, he heard a familiar booming voice coming from the front of the room.

"Sledddd!"

Without even looking to see who it was that gave the shout-out, Dickie knew instantly that Reggie Oliver was on the scene. It was Oliver who hung the Sled Dog nickname on Dickie. On a night when Oliver was being honored as a hall of fame inductee, he made sure that Dickie would know that he had not been forgotten about. "When Reggie yelled out *Sled,* it made me feel a lot more at ease," Dickie said. "When I went back (to Marshall) all those years ago, things felt spooky and weird. It was sad because I knew my teammates wouldn't be there. But now, things for me are much better than they were ten, fifteen years ago."

Dickie's football career didn't end the way he wanted. Still, he has no regrets about playing for the Thundering Herd. And while he's not likely to come back for any homecoming celebrations, he doesn't mind providing some personal insights about his playing days at MU. A few years back, he wrote a letter to a former schoolmate. In that letter he wrote about the lessons learned from his college experience. Here's an excerpt:

> I've always been glad that I picked Marshall. I learned a lot of lessons . . . but the hardest lesson I had to learn was how quick your life can change. I have had many events to cross my path since the crash, but there hasn't been anything that has affected my life that equals the magnitude of losing my teammates. Life has so many lessons to teach us. But I have found the most important one. It doesn't matter what team we may be on in life. When God calls our number the game is over.

Chapter Seven

Moving On

Even though I was no longer a college athlete, I still couldn't make a clean disconnect from the game. Going home to Jacksonville for Thanksgiving in 1970 was a strange experience. I was surprised to hear from friends that they didn't expect to see me again. Most of what folks knew about my football days at Marshall was based on a story from the summer of '69 that ran in the Jacksonville paper. The report summarized my freshman season in college and how I was expected to compete for a starting position in Marshall's secondary as a sophomore. Since it was my junior year, people assumed that I was still playing, which meant that I was probably on that plane.

When I returned to school after the holiday break, I never thought I'd be writing about the crash as part of my coursework as a journalism major. Since the crash was a major story, I thought that only the more experienced j-majors would draw writing assignments related to the crash. That semester, I served as a staff writer for *The Parthenon*. I was assigned to write a story on the National Transportation Safety Board panel of inquiry that conducted a federal hearing on the crash. It was a front-page story, and I still have a copy of that edition from all those Decembers ago.

At the time of the crash, it had been nearly one year since I played football. As far as I was concerned, I was far removed from the team. There was never a time that I felt any urge to put the pads on again. That's why, *at that time*, I never thought much about the possibility that I could have been on that DC-9 jet that night.

In the post-crash atmosphere, there was an air of uncertainty about the future of football at Marshall. But even then, I always believed the program would continue. There were too many school administrators and coaches (who were not on the plane) who wanted to keep football, and they didn't mind starting from scratch. Another plus for the program was the shared proceeds received from Wichita State's national telethon, which featured Bill Cosby, Monte Hall, George Goble, and other luminaries.

For the three remaining coaches on the MU staff—Mickey Jackson, Carl Kokor, and Red Dawson—it was touch and go. "After the Ohio game was called off, the big question was whether there would even be a next season," Jackson said. "Nobody really knew what direction it would go. We sat in the office day by day trying to determine if the school would keep the football program going."

Reggie Oliver, the likely starter at quarterback, never doubted that Marshall would keep football. Oliver was confident because winter workouts started as they always had at the beginning of the new semester in January. These workouts served as a preseason conditioner for spring football in March and April. And besides, it wasn't like the school didn't have any players to replace the ones who died. "The varsity was gone," he said, "but we still had a core of players to start with (from the freshman team)."

All concerns about Marshall ditching football were quickly put to rest when Joe McMullen came onboard as the new athletics director. As a former assistant coach under Joe Paterno at Penn State, McMullen had deep football roots. The vacant coaching position attracted a fair amount of interest. It was no secret that Sam Huff, a West Virginia native and NFL legend, wanted the job. Huff had the pedigree and name recognition to do well in recruiting. But for whatever reason, none of that really mattered. Huff never even got an interview. Dick Bestwick, a Georgia Tech assistant coach, was eventually named as Tolley's successor.

It was only temporary.

Bestwick changed his mind and opted to go back to the Yellow Jackets after only *two days* on the job. The coaching situation was finally settled in mid-March of '71 when Jack Lengyel of Wooster College (Ohio) was hired.

In a way, I felt obligated to put the pads on again since I had played with most of the guys who died. So I made a comeback of sorts during spring drills, which signaled the return of football only five months after the tragedy. On that first day of practice, it was such an awkward feeling to leave the locker room at Fairfield Stadium and run down the ramp onto the field. It took about a week or so for me to feel reasonably comfortable.

This group of athletes was vastly different from what I encountered during my first two seasons as a player. Even though I had not played the game in nearly eighteen months, I had as much or more varsity experience than everyone else except for the three players who missed the flight. This squad was comprised of players from the freshman team and a cast of walk-ons that included soccer, baseball, and basketball players who decided to come out and see what they could do on the gridiron. Some played football in high school; others had zilch experience.

In some instances, the inexperience of these novices could have led to unnecessary injuries. During a scrimmage, one of the basketball players learning how to play tight end ran a post route and stretched out for a pass that was badly overthrown. He was lean at six feet, seven inches, and totally exposed, ripe for a vicious hit. But I held back. He had not yet learned how to protect himself and I knew it. Anyway, the pass wasn't even catchable.

From a coaching standpoint, a different approach was needed to get the maximum out of a group that had hardly any game experience under its collective belt. To successfully compete against veteran teams, Marshall's youngsters would have to toughen up and grow up real fast.

"We didn't know how far we could push them," Jackson said. "You had to be encouraging and supportive. There's a fine line between pushing a kid to make him better as opposed to driving a kid into the ground and running him off. That was the real difficult part about coaching this group. We had to make day-to-day adjustments in our coaching style."

Spring drills, in those days, culminated with the annual Varsity-Alumni game, which always resulted in a no-sweat victory for the Varsity. This time, though, winning—even against a group of out-of-shape ex-jocks who hadn't played the game in years—was not viewed as a sure thing. The Alumni, which had fifty players to sign up for the game, were confident they could provide some stiff competition.

Given the team's overall lack of experience, nobody knew what to expect. A larger than usual crowd of about 5,000 showed up to take a closer look at Marshall University's work-in-progress. The Thundering Herd won 26-0, which eased some of the anxiety among the coaching staff.

"If the coaches had that feeling (that we might lose to the Alumni), I never sensed that as a player," said Ed Carter. "They (Alumni) had good players but they hadn't played the game in several years and they were not in (football) shape."

It was nearly ten years after the '71 spring game that I learned how much of a difference there is between being in decent physical condition and being fit for football. After my discharge from the air force, I returned to Marshall for graduate school and signed up to play for the Alumni in one of those spring games in the early 1980s. What a difference a decade makes! I saw the plays as they developed and knew what to do, but unfortunately my reaction time was way off. I felt like I was moving in slow motion compared to the younger players on the other side of the ball.

As for the Varsity-Alumni game in '71, I got really pumped up emotionally. What really got me going was one of the coaches on the '68 freshman team, Jim "Hillbilly" Preston, who lined up at offensive guard that night. All game long, my former coach kept jawing away, and I let him get inside my head. Eventually, I got tired of it, and I slammed my right hand into his face mask. It was a solid blow. But after the game, I found out that the dull pain I felt in my hand was the by-product of a bone fracture.

The motivational factor in Varsity-Alumni games is very different for each team. It's serious business for the Varsity. How you perform during the spring sets the tone for where you end up on the depth chart at the start of preseason drills in August. For the Alumni, it's like a reunion. Players come back to enjoy each other's company and reminisce. It wasn't unusual to look over at the Alumni sideline and see players swigging down a brew or two during the course of the game.

The spring football contest tended to be one-sided in favor of the Varsity. Players for the Alumni team are hard pressed to hold their own for four quarters against young college players who have practiced as a unit for four weeks

Except for the first day of spring practice, I didn't think about the crash all that much. That was hardly the case when I arrived at the stadium to get dressed for the Varsity-Alumni game. The team manager issued uniforms and he handed me No. 40, the jersey worn by Larry "Dupree" Sanders, the Thundering Herd's best defensive back. Dupree and I were partners in the secondary in our first two seasons of college ball.

I admit that I was in a state of disbelief when the jersey was handed to me. The more I looked at it, the more uneasy I felt about wearing it. It just didn't seem right. And besides, I didn't even request it. My jersey number from the 1969 season was already spoken for by Felix Jordan, and that was fine. I didn't want to make an issue of it, so I accepted the jersey and kept my thoughts to myself.

In the waning minutes of the Varsity-Alumni game, the defense trotted off the field. I looked up in the stands and saw Sanders's girlfriend, Macie Lugo, standing on the front row. Studying her facial expression, it was clear that, for her, watching Marshall's No. 40 on a football field evoked fond but painful memories from her very recent past. She yelled out to me with a rhyme, "Hey! Craig Teeee, number for-teeee!"

Unsure as to how to respond, I waved and smiled and kept my silence.

The start of fall practice in 1971 was a special time. Since the NCAA had given Marshall a special exemption allowing freshmen to play varsity, the excitement level was off the charts. With over 90 percent of the team made up of freshmen and sophomores, the team was renamed the "Young Thundering Herd."

My comeback as a player lasted until the early weeks of preseason practice. After losing my starting position to transfer Gene Nance, I decided not to play anymore. Nance has some serious football genes. His older brother Jim starred at Syracuse University and enjoyed a solid pro career, mostly with the Boston Patriots of the old American Football League, which eventually became the New England Patriots of the NFL.

The genetics of the Nance family, however, had nothing to do with my lack of competitive drive. I never had any second thoughts about quitting football for the second time in twenty-two months. Call it ego. I had no desire to sit and watch, and I wasn't motivated nearly enough to prove that I could play my way back into the starting lineup.

The fall of '71 wasn't any different from November '69 when I quit the team. Football just wasn't in me. No heart for the game. Even though I'd been an athlete since junior high school, I knew I wouldn't miss football to the point where I'd want to give it one more go. That's when I knew I was immune to any withdrawal symptoms. I never thought I'd feel that way in my early 20s. Observing the game as a spectator was okay with me.

There were no issues for me in owning up to the reality that my days as a college athlete were over. After the fall of '71 (the season following the crash), I stopped going to home games and never listened to road games on the radio. But it didn't take long for me to discover that I still could not get Marshall football completely out of my system.

About eighteen months before my college graduation, I looked for a new apartment and ended up moving to a house located on the same street as Fairfield Stadium. At the time I looked at the newspaper ad about the place, I had no idea that it was located *across the street.* Talk about close proximity. I could walk across the street and be at one of the entrance gates in a matter of minutes. The house was divided into three apartments. From my bedroom window on the third floor, I had a reasonably decent view of the action taking place inside Fairfield. The scoreboard blocked some of that view. But for the most part, I could see enough to tell what was going on and could hear the announcer just as if I was actually sitting in the stands. It was like me having a free ticket for every home game.

I never had any regrets about leaving the game. It's funny though. My life as an athlete did not end like I hoped it would. That's probably why I never thought much about becoming a sports writer. Once I got my journalism degree, I was sure that I would be more inclined to gravitate toward writing news, features, and commentaries. As things turned out, I eventually reconnected to sports as a journalist/photographer who has covered athletics at every level.

During the fall of '71, the most memorable highlight was being a witness to Marshall's reverberating upset win over Xavier University (Ohio). That game holds special significance. It was the school's first home game since the 1970 season as well as its first victory after the crash.

Fairfield Stadium was filled to the brim with a then-record crowd of 13,000 on hand to check out the Herd. Marshall, which wasn't expected to win a game that year, did not disappoint. Xavier was the heavy favorite to win by a landslide, but the game did not play out that way.

Nobody knew what to expect. The Herd held its own the previous week in a 29-6 loss to Morehead State University. Xavier was supposed to be much better than Morehead. The Musketeers opened their season with a ten-point road loss to perennial MAC contender Miami of Ohio. Not even the most die-hard MU fans expected a victory. On paper, the home team was overmatched because of having to play so many freshmen. But in many people's minds, victory had already been achieved before kickoff. The fact that Marshall had assembled a team that competed and scored a touchdown in its season opener a week earlier was reason enough for optimism.

This match-up was fiercely contested from the very start. Soccer-player-turned placekicker Blake Smith booted a thirty-one-yard field goal on the final play of the first quarter to give Marshall a surprising 3-0 lead that held up through halftime. Xavier rallied to go up 13-9 late in the fourth quarter, but there was still a glimmer of hope. Time was running out, but the home team was still in it. The Thundering Herd was primed to show everybody that, even though Xavier was on top, this game was far from being over.

With one minute and eighteen seconds left to play, Marshall put together a drive that would ultimately deliver victory on the final play of the game.

The defense held Xavier to a three and out to force a punt and the Herd got the ball near midfield. From this point on, the drama escalated with every play. Could this group of young and untested tenderfoots manufacture a way to win a game that nobody thought they had any chance of winning? During that final drive, Marshall converted a couple of fourth downs to keep the chains moving. The clock kept ticking. There was still a reasonable chance for a Marshall miracle.

Sitting in the corner bleachers of the end zone, I had a full view of the game's winning play as it developed. The play worked to perfection because freshman receiver Lanny Steed was close to unstoppable that day. Steed, who finished with eight catches for 113 yards, torched Xavier's secondary all game long, mostly on medium-range post patterns.

The ball rested on Xavier's thirteen-yard line. As Reggie Oliver came to the line of scrimmage, the game clock was now ticking off the seconds in single digits.

Nine seconds.

Eight seconds.

Seven seconds.

Oliver wanted to be sure that everybody was set before the ball was snapped. His team needed to avoid getting flagged for a penalty at this critical juncture. The Marshall sideline was frantic. Coaches, players, and everyone else, it seemed, kept yelling for Oliver to get the ball snapped.

Three seconds.

Two seconds . . .

"Hut, hut!"

Oliver took the snap and then the final gun was fired. It was the last play, winner take all. If the Herd failed, it would be another discouraging defeat. If the Herd scored, this play would go down as one of the most memorable in college football annals.

Oliver faked a handoff, rolled slightly to his right, looked for Jerry Arrasmith in the corner of the end zone, and then eyeballed Steed over the middle. The defense reacted to Steed's presence, but, as things turned out, the Musketeers had been suckered. Oliver wheeled in the opposite direction and floated a pass to running back Terry Gardner, who had drifted out of the backfield to the left side. Meanwhile, the defense paid little attention to offensive tackle Jack Crabtree who had pulled out to the left to block for Gardner as he made the catch.

With so much focus on stopping Steed, the left side was wide open and there was only one Musketeer in the immediate vicinity. Crabtree promptly leveled the lone defender and Gardner galloped to the end zone.

Touchdown, Herd!

Marshall 15, Xavier 13.

Fairfield Stadium erupted with a seismic roar. Frenzied fans stampeded their way onto the field like a runaway horde of African wildebeests.

It's evident that there were some folks at Marshall who had faith in the Young Herd's ability to accomplish what the vast majority believed to be impossible. In the days leading up to the '71 home opener, signs, bed sheets, and posters conveying messages of encouragement to the football team littered the campus.

There was one sign, however, that stood out more than others. It was placed on an outside wall near an entrance to one of the men's dormitories.

At the top of the display, the headline read, SUPPORT THE YOUNG HERD . . .

A jockey strap taped to the wall was positioned underneath the top headline.

The bottom headline, in smaller letters, read, GIVE XAVIER A YOUNG THUNDERING HERNIA.

Was this a case of prophecy coming to pass? We'll never know for sure. What we do know is that Xavier never recovered from the Marshall miracle. As things turned out, it was the beginning stages of a long and agonizing downhill slide for the Musketeers, who lost eight in a row and finished their season at 1-9.

The Marshall-Xavier contest in '71 was a classic in every sense of the word. Oliver's touchdown toss to Gardner made ESPN's Top 100 Plays. It ranks eighty-third on the network's list of the most thrilling plays in the history of college football.

Nobody who was at Fairfield Stadium on that day will ever forget what they saw. For at least two hours *after the game*, a crowd of three thousand, maybe four thousand, hung out at the stadium to savor the moment. Some were teary-eyed. Some were whooping and hollering as if they had won millions in a Publishers Clearing House Sweepstakes. Coming out of the locker room after a shower and getting dressed, Coach Jackson remembered the scene all too well: "The celebration seemed like it lasted the rest of the evening," he said. "We came back out and (looking at the size of the crowd still in the stands) it looked like the fourth quarter of a football game."

This was a satisfying, exhilarating, and spirit-lifting win. But the game also served as a fitting tribute to honor those who perished in the plane crash the previous year. Marshall did win one other game that season, a 12-10 homecoming victory over Bowling Green.

The '71 football team deserves mountains of applause and appreciation. This group labored under dire circumstances and held together at a time when the program could have easily folded. It would've been nice for me to be part of that. But at that time in my college life, I had other priorities, and football wasn't one of them. Earnestine and I were married and our firstborn, a son, was on the way. Carlos Greenlee arrived in July, four days before my twenty-first birthday. Being a husband and father, however, had nothing to do with me leaving the team prior to the start of the '71 season. Even now, it's so surprising that I received an invite to a reunion of the '71 team a few years ago.

I declined the invitation and responded with a letter specifying my reasons for doing so. I was not on the team when the '71 season began. Sure, I was a starter that previous spring, played in the Varsity-Alumni game, and was on the roster in the preseason. But when I decided to walk away from the game for good, I felt like I forfeited any claim of being a team member for that year. Neither injuries nor off-the-field shenanigans had anything to do with me quitting. It was simply the right time for me to bow out and move on. Had I actually been on the team during the fall, when the games that really count are played, then I could rightfully take my place as a legitimate member of Marshall University's Young Thundering Herd.

The airplane crash, coupled with a countless number of consecutive futile seasons, could have put Herd football in a long-lasting holding pattern. Eventually brighter days would come, but progress was not an overnight occurrence. It would take more than a decade after the Xavier game before the Marshall faithful could see clear signs of a resurrected program primed for stardom.

Check out this list of Marshall milestones that occurred after that history-making victory in September '71:

- 1984—Hallelujah! Marshall finishes at 6-5 and closes out the year with back-to-back victories (both on the road) to secure its first winning season in twenty years.
- 1987—The Herd advances to the NCAA Division I-AA championship game but suffers a heart-breaking 43-42 loss to the University of Northeast Louisiana.
- 1991—The team in green returns to the 1-AA title game, but still no cigar. Marshall falls 25-17 to Youngstown State University.
- 1992—The Herd nails down its first national championship in dramatic fashion. With less than ten seconds left in the game, Willy Merrick kicks the first and only field goal of his college career (a twenty-two-yarder) to propel Marshall to a 31-28 win over nemesis Youngstown State.
- 1993—Marshall hooks up with Youngstown in a title match-up for the third consecutive year. The third time is not a charm. The Penguins prevail by a count of 17-5.
- 1995—The national championship trophy eludes Marshall one more time in a 22-20 loss to the University of Montana.
- 1996—This proved to be the year for the Herd to bring thunder. Marshall goes 15-0 and spanks Montana 49-29 to win its second national championship trophy in five years. Newcomer Randy Moss sets NCAA single-season records for most touchdown catches and receiving yards by a freshman.
- 1997—Marshall returns to the Mid-American Conference after being out of sight and out of mind for twenty-eight years. The Herd beats the University of Toledo in the conference championship contest to earn the school's first bowl bid in fifty years. Marshall plays well but drops a 34-31 squeaker to the University of Mississippi in the closing moments of the Motor City Bowl. Moss finished the year with twenty-five touchdown catches to establish a new NCAA single-season mark. Additionally, he won the Biletnikoff Award, which goes to the nation's top receiver, and he was also a finalist in the Heisman voting. Quarterback Chad Pennington led the nation with thirty-nine touchdown passes.

- 1998—Billy Malashevich kicked a game-winning field goal with time running out as MU upset South Carolina 24-21. The Herd (12-1) returned to the post-season and stuffed Louisville 48-29 in the Motor City Bowl.
- 1999—Posted a stunning 13-10 road victory over ACC powerhouse Clemson at Death Valley. Pennington and company did what was needed in Marshall's 21-3 drubbing of Brigham Young University in the Motor City Bowl. Pennington ended his college career ranked among the NCAA's top five in passing yards, touchdown passes, and completions.
- 2000—Marshall lost three regular-season games but recovered in time to win seven of its last eight. Took home another Motor City Bowl trophy by beating the University of Cincinnati 25-14.
- 2001—Quarterback Byron Leftwich brought Marshall back to life after his team trailed East Carolina by thirty points at the half in the GMAC Bowl. Leftwich ran for a score and completed 41 of 70 passes for 576 yards and four touchdowns as the Herd rallied to take a 64-61 win in double overtime. Not only was this the highest-scoring contest in the history of bowl games, it also represented the largest deficit that any winning team had to overcome.
- 2002—Marshall takes fifth MAC title in six seasons; beats Louisville 38-15 in the GMAC Bowl.
- 2009—Seven-year bowl drought ends when Marshall gets invited to the Little Caesar's Pizza Bowl. Late-game interception enables the Herd to hold off rival Ohio University in a 21-17 victory. The win pushed Marshall (7-6) past the break-even point for the season.

Former Marshall coach Mickey Jackson is convinced that '71 was the year that the cornerstone was laid for MU football. He believes that had the program folded at that time, the Herd would not have reached the levels it has. "If Marshall had not continued football, but waited ten, fifteen, or twenty years (to bring the sport back), it would have been like starting from ground zero," he explained. "There would've been no momentum whatsoever. Because the school kept the program going, it continued to build and build."

The restoration process at MU got a huge boost in '71. The NCAA granted an exemption that allowed freshmen to play varsity football for the Thundering Herd. This special exemption was for Marshall only. The school's unique status, however, didn't last for very long. The NCAA rescinded its freshman eligibility rule in '72. As a result, freshmen at all NCAA-member schools were given the green light to play football and basketball at the varsity level.

Was it coincidence that the NCAA axed its eligibility requirements only one year after Marshall was granted special permission to play freshmen? One could argue that the Herd's success in recruiting and retaining its athletes in '71 may have had some bearing on the NCAA's change of heart. That's highly unlikely. At the time the exemption was given to MU, the issue of freshman eligibility had already been added to the list of proposed rules changes being considered by the NCAA. Even so, Marshall will always hold the distinction of being the first school in the country to hold its own against varsity competition with a mostly freshmen squad.

"That freshman class of '71 showed that it could be done," said Oliver. "That was the team that laid the bricks for the foundation of what was to come later on."

MU's Deep Defenders Among Best Sophs in Country—Tolley

By LOWELL CADE

Advertiser Sports Writer

Pass defense hasn't been one of Marshall's strong suits in football over the years, and especially during the past two.

And, this year it looks like Coach Rick Tolley will intrust the responsibility to three sophomores — Larry Sanders, Craig Greenlee and Nathanial (Nat) Ruffin. But don't sell this trio short.

"I'd stack them up against the best sophomores in major college football," said Tolley this week.

Last year the MU secondary was fifth among Mid-American Conference teams in pass defense, giving up an average of 127 yards per game, and nine touchdowns. The Herd defenders picked off 11 enemy aerials. Graduated Joe Ralbusky and departed Mike Smith led the way in numbers with three apiece.

10 Interceptions

In five freshmen games last year, the Little Herd pass defenders picked off 10 enemy aerials, and Greenlee led the pack with four.

Greenlee's a 6-0, 166-pounder from Jacksonville, Fla. Ruffin is 5-11, 176 from Quincy, Fla., and Sanders, 6-1, 195, is from Tuscaloosa, Ala.

All are versatile performers. Due to a recent outbreak of minor injuries on the offense to receivers, Tolley has had to press all three into service as backup duty at flanker and split end.

Tolley says he feels Ohio State couldn't have three better sophomores on the field. "I know there are better veteran defensive backs," he said. "Experience means a lot. But these sophomores have good speed, range and are good tackles. In short, they have a lot of potential. But, they're sophomores and they're apt to make sophomore mistakes."

* * *

Thursday the Herd, even the coaches, welcomed the end of two-a-day drills. Classes begin Monday and practice time has been set for 3 p. m. Saturday even the Herd will work out at Fairfield Stadium before only Big Green Club members and faculty. Today's one workout was also set for 3 o'clock.

The coaches made one line-

CRAIG GREENLEE
Sophomore safety

up change Thursday when sophomore Willie Bluford was promoted to No. 1 fullback ahead of junior Dick Carter.

"He's one of the most improved players we have," said Tolley. "He looks faster than he did last spring, he's making fewer mistakes, running hard and blocking well. On top of that he's a great kid with a fine attitude."

Here's a preseason article on the Thundering Herd's all-sophomore secondary that was published on September 12, 1969, in the *Huntington Advertiser*. Marshall fans were excited about the upcoming season because of the sophomores who played on the '68 freshman team that finished the season undefeated.

Bob Wright (left) and John Shellcroft (right) take over the podium from Marshall President Roland Nelson during the black student protest in the fall of 1969.
(Photo: The Parthenon/Marshall University)

Black students stand together as a symbol of unity during the
protest.
(Photo: Chief Justice yearbook/Marshall University)

Craig T. Greenlee comes to the sidelines in agony after tackling the bruising fullback from the University of Toledo. *(Photo: The Parthenon/Marshall University)*

Three Students Hurt In Fight

Three Marshall University students were injured Friday in a fight which started shortly after the finish of a football game between a fraternity and a non-Greek student organization on the university's intramural field, city police reported.

Police made no arrests in the 5:40 p.m. incident.

Taken to the Chesapeake & Ohio Railway Hospital were Donald H. Saller, 20, of 1434 5th Ave., John Onderko, 20, of 1533 4th Ave., and Charles Ward, 19, of 723 W. 18th St.

Mr. Saller was admitted in satisfactory condition with a severe cut of the right chest while the other two were treated for smaller multiple cuts and released. Police said knives were apparently used.

One of the victims reported being struck over the head with a bottle and the others said they were jumped from behind by about five subjects as they were walking away from the field.

Above is a replication of a newspaper article about the melee that could have easily escalated into a bloody race riot on Marshall's campus. This news brief ran in the *Herald-Advertiser* on November 14, 1970. That evening, the football team's plane went down and the impact of this story was significantly diminished.

This photo of the author was featured in the documentary *Ashes to Glory* by mistake. *(Photo: Herald-Dispatch)*

A bronze memorial for the crash victims is mounted on the wall of the westside entrance to Joan C. Edwards Stadium, which is the home field for Marshall's Thundering Herd football team. *(Photo by Craig T. Greenlee)*

Board named to hold hearing on plane crash

By CRAIG T. GREENLEE
Staff reporter

A four-man board of inquiry has been named to conduct a federal hearing here Dec. 14 into the Nov. 14 airplane crash that took the lives of 75 persons, including most of the MU football team, several coaches, officials, and supporters.

Edward Slattery, director of the office of public affairs of the National Transportation Safety Board, told The Parthenon Tuesday from his Washington office that the hearing panel would include Oscar Laurel,

final report will begin," said Slattery.

"It will take a while to give the results of the findings of the board because the process is extremely thorough and very meticulous. I don't expect that the findings of the board be completed before April."

In discussing witnesses that will be questioned at the hearing, Slattery said, "a list of the witnesses will not be released until the morning of the hearing," he said.

"Anyone who thinks that they may know something that may be of help will have to contact Richard Rodriguez in

The author, who majored in journalism at Marshall, wrote the above article about the federal investigation of the crash. The story appeared on the front page of the school's student newspaper, *The Parthenon.*

A granite cenotaph stands as a lasting tribute at the team's memorial site at Spring Hill Cemetery in Huntington, West Virginia. *(Photo: Craig T. Greenlee)*

Chapter Eight

Etched in Memory

The personal turmoil caused by the plane crash was immeasurable. Nobody was immune from feeling the awful sting of a shocking reality. Death had claimed the lives of so many, all in one swoop. And even worse was that it happened in such a horrific manner. Many of the deceased were our peers at Marshall. Like us, they had visions, hopes, and dreams for a wondrous future. But it just wasn't to be. Death deprived our schoolmates of pursuing their desired destinies.

For those who lost boyfriends, childhood buddies, or best friends, the pain and agony was far more intense than it was for others. If the crash had never happened, those friendships would probably have lasted a lifetime. Here are their stories.

*   *   *

It was early afternoon on November 13, a few hours before the football team would leave campus to go to the airport. Macie Lugo and her boyfriend Larry "Dupree" Sanders savored some *alone* time in a lounge area known as "the pit." This popular spot for couples, located in Twin Towers girls' dorm where Macie lived, had no television sets.

The pit lounge was a sunken area about two steps lower than the rest of the dorm's ground floor where the lobby, front desk, TV lounge, and elevators were located. Cozy but not private, this area was roomy enough to seat about twenty people. It had a couple of entrances that doubled as exits that were connected to two walls about five and a half feet high. The height of the walls prevented most people from seeing if the pit was occupied. Most basketball players (six feet, three inches or taller) could look over the wall and see. Everybody else had to walk to one of the entrances to get an unobstructed view. The lighting level was always soft and subdued, which enhanced the romantic ambience.

Right after Dupree left the pit that day, Macie noticed a dime on the carpet. She's not sure if the coin came out of Dupree's pockets. Ever since that day, she associates dimes with Larry Sanders. It's a reminder. "It's his way of letting me know that he's always there, that he's always watching out for me," she said.

Emotionally, Macie had more than enough to deal with by the time she arrived in Alabama for the funeral. Dupree and his family were on her mind, but that wasn't Macie's sole focus. She couldn't help but feel the pain and anguish felt by the families of Robert VanHorn, Freddy Wilson, and Joe Hood. "All I could think about was how great a loss it was," Macie recalled about the joint funeral for her boyfriend and his three friends. "It was so sad, for me and for the families. I had a great concern for their loss as well as the grief that I was feeling."

November 1970 was supposed to be a happy time. Macie was looking forward to Thanksgiving break. She was full of anticipation after she invited Dupree to come home with her to Bluefield, West Virginia, to meet her parents and spend the holiday with her family. He had not made a firm commitment to visit Bluefield, which annoyed Macie. Dupree told her he was thinking about going home to Alabama since he had not seen *his* parents in a long time. Back then, it was considered a major step for a guy to accompany his girlfriend to her hometown for Thanksgiving or Christmas. Doing so was a sign that the relationship had grown way beyond casual dating. Dupree and Macie were viewed as a "serious" couple.

Macie learned later—while she was in Tuscaloosa for the funerals—that Dupree had a surprise for her. When Macie met members of her boyfriend's family for the first time, one of the relatives, a sister-in-law, pulled Macie to the side for a private conversation.

"I've got something to tell you, Macie."

"Oh, okay. What is it?"

"We talked to Dupree a few weeks ago. He told us then that he wouldn't be home for Thanksgiving because he was going to be in Bluefield with you."

Dupree had purposely kept Macie in suspense about his holiday plans.

"I didn't have any idea," she said, "until I was there for his funeral."

Macie would meet Dupree's sister-in-law again. This time it was after the funeral and at a place where she didn't expect an encounter. On the return flight from Alabama to West Virginia, Macie and Murrial Jarrett (who accompanied Macie to Tuscaloosa) had a layover in Atlanta, Georgia. As they sat and talked, they noticed a couple of familiar-looking figures headed their way from the other end of the concourse. As these people got closer, they recognized it was Dupree's oldest brother and his wife. They stopped by to see Macie and Murrial before it was time for them to board the plane for West Virginia. Macie didn't know the couple lived in Atlanta.

"She (Dupree's sister-in-law) hugged me and embraced me," Macie said. "I don't remember them saying they would come see us (at the airport). What a gift that was. She was able to feel my personal struggle and pain and she comforted me. That showed me that she valued me as a person."

It took a few weeks after the tragedy before Macie could muster up enough desire to talk about her innermost feelings. She was seeking an attentive ear. Instead, the words Macie heard left her feeling numb to her bones. It was like getting doused in the face with a bucket-full of ice-cold water.

"It's about time that we moved on from that (plane crash)," she was told.

The statement was harsh and insensitive. Even more hurtful—this bit of advice came from a trusted confidant. Macie will not reveal that person's identity.

This was strange. Macie always assumed the role of caretaker in family and personal relationships. Now the roles were reversed. *She* was the one who needed someone to listen to what she had to say. But there was no one to turn to. "With all the trauma I went through, that's what I was told (when I wanted to talk)," she said. "So, I just shored up and put on this face. I kept a stiff upper lip and went on."

A surprising comment from Macie's father made matters worse. Earl Lugo felt compelled to weigh in on his daughter's color choices for her wardrobe. Macie preferred blue and black.

"You need to stop wearing so much black," Earl Lugo advised. "You are not a widow." That was an odd statement coming from a man who earned his living as a mortician, Macie thought. "I guess he felt I should hurry up and get on with my life," she said. "He'd tell me, 'People die, and they're buried, and you just move on.'"

Macie's personal experience taught her that there is no right way or wrong way to grieve. She believes that whenever someone suffers a loss of any kind (death, divorce, or job for example), he or she should grieve. If not, the person risks putting himself or herself in emotionally unhealthy situations. Macie readily acknowledged that she didn't deal with her deep-seated feelings in a timely manner. As a result, she made some inappropriate decisions in relationships, her choice of friends, and career opportunities. "I do have regrets that I let some wonderful (career) opportunities slip away," she said. "Emotionally, I didn't deal with it. I just shut down and locked it all away in a compartment (in my mind). The pain and the sense of longing and loss were always present. Getting through the rest of the school year was like a prolonged death march. It seemed like the days would never end."

Aside from keeping her head in the books, Macie had no interest in doing much of anything. Going out on weekends was not on her *to do* list. Her outlook changed to some extent because of Reggie Oliver, who was hurting as much as anyone. Oliver lost four of his friends in the crash, one of whom was Larry Sanders.

Macie had no plans to go anywhere other than the confines of Twin Towers dorm. So she was floored when Oliver stopped by on weekends, and he wasn't alone. Oliver was *accompanied by his date* and armed with persuasive reasoning to convince Macie to join them for a night out. Oliver went beyond requesting her presence, he insisted on it. His desire was for Macie to have some semblance of a social life. She will never forget the gesture.

"Reggie wasn't going to let me sit around the dorm every weekend," Macie said. "There I was—somebody who was either grieving or trying not to grieve, or pretending not to grieve—going out with a friend. And then there's the other lady who's thinking she's going out on a date with the quarterback of the football team, but she ends up being part of this kind of deal. It was a new definition for a threesome."

Oliver believed that if Macie had not been encouraged, she could have easily gotten very comfortable being a recluse. To his way of thinking, it just wasn't right. After all, Macie was Marshall's black homecoming queen for '70. She won the Miss Black Pearl pageant, had her own float in the school's homecoming parade, and was honored during halftime of the homecoming game along with Miss Marshall and her court.

"You knew there was a void in people's lives because of the plane crash," said Oliver. "All of us were going through the same thing. I did what I did, hoping it would create some sense of normalcy. There was a need to provide an outlet for people who needed support, a shoulder to cry on, somebody to talk to. It was an effort to help prevent one of our schoolmates from possibly slipping into a depressive state. In Macie's case, it was even more special because Macie was Dupree's girlfriend and Dupree was my home boy."

When it came time for the Varsity-Alumni game in the spring of '71, Oliver would not be available for a night out with Macie. He was playing in that game. Quite frankly, it would not have come as a huge surprise if Macie had opted to not go to the game. Nobody could blame her if she had. It had only been five months since that horrible November night. You could only imagine just how vivid the recollections were for those who were romantically involved with the players who died that night.

Macie did not put herself on self-imposed lockdown on the weekend of that game. Instead, she chose to be part of the anticipation and excitement at Fairfield Stadium. It was the first football game since the tragedy. "I wanted to come out and show my support for the guys who were out there to carry on," she said.

The Varsity-Alumni game of '71 was the last time Macie would ever attend a Marshall football game in person. That's not to imply that she was turned off from football in particular or sports in general because of the plane crash. She keeps tabs on the Herd on a regular basis via the newspapers and television.

The summer of '71 was decision time for Macie, who had just completed her sophomore year at Marshall. She considered staying but decided she'd be better off elsewhere. Attending Howard University was one possibility. Instead, she opted to go back home. Earl Lugo made an attractive offer that she couldn't turn down.

In exchange for Macie helping out with the family business (funeral home) and her younger sisters, her father paid all of her college expenses. Macie transferred to Bluefield State College and graduated in '72 with a degree in teacher's education. "I needed a change," Macie said of her decision to go back home. "Nothing was ever the same for me (after the crash). The relationships with the people Dupree and I used to hang out with changed when he died. Interactions were different. Some people felt uncomfortable. They didn't know what to say. It was time to move on. I needed to be in another environment."

Even though Macie had no desire to come back for a Marshall homecoming, she still made frequent visits to campus—for family-related reasons.

Macie has a nephew, Mark, who suffers from autism and lives in a group home in Huntington. Mark spent much of his time at the West Virginia Autism Training Center from the time he was nine years old until he turned seventeen. The center, which is housed on the Marshall campus, provides education, training, and treatment for West Virginians who have autism or similar disorders. Macie, who lives near Charleston, West Virginia, frequently stopped by to visit Mark and offer her support.

Whenever Macie came to visit Mark, she could never ignore the visual reminders about her days at Marshall. To get to the Autism Center, she had to walk past the plaza area of the Memorial Student Union where the Memorial Fountain stands. The fountain is a tulip-shaped sculpture built in '72 as a tribute to those who perished in the crash.

The fountain has seventy-five points at its top. Each point represents the life of each person who was a passenger on that ill-fated flight. For most of the year, the fountain's waters flow freely. The school has an annual service to honor the memories of the victims on the anniversary of the tragedy. After November 14, the water is cut off for the winter. The fountain's waters flow once more when spring arrives, signifying rebirth, renewal, and the continuation of life.

Macie always made her visits during the winter months, so all she ever saw was a non-flowing fountain. "It was kind of depressing to not see the flowing of the water, realizing what it means and entails," she confessed. "But I'm glad that they still remember November 14 every year. They still honor the players from that time, and that's very special."

Macie, a personal care assistant who doubles as a substitute school teacher, got an unexpected opportunity to share the life lessons she learned about dealing with difficult times. She was assigned to an anatomy class at Charleston High School. Most of the students in class that day were freshmen and sophomores who played on the school's basketball team. The regular teacher and some of the other students in that class were out of town to witness the presidential inauguration of Barack Obama in Washington, DC. There was only one bus available for that trip. As a result, a large number of students who wanted to go to DC had to stay home, and they weren't happy about that.

The basketball players in the class, Macie learned, had other issues on their minds. They were despondent about a losing streak they were going through. Losing was a foreign concept to this group. At every level—middle school, YMCA, AAU—they always prevailed. Now that they were high school athletes, winning was no longer automatic, and they struggled in coming to grips with losing.

Macie recognized that *this* was a teaching moment. "You deal with the subject matter (for that particular class)," she said. "But life issues are also subject matter."

Macie the teacher used sports as a vehicle to get and keep the athletes' attention. Sports, she pointed out, has always been an effective way for her to communicate with guys. Now that she had established a comfort level with her audience, Macie proceeded to speak and provide a perspective the class members had never heard:

> Guys, listen to me. Your outside shot could be beyond the NBA three-point line and you could be Stevie Wonder and still make the shot. You could be an Honor Roll student and be dating the school's homecoming queen. You can have all the Kobe (Bryant) and LeBron (James) game jerseys and travel places to see your favorite pro teams play. These are signs that life is good.
>
> But that's not the time when the most beneficial information comes. It comes when you're losing, when you're faced with adverse circumstances. Those are the situations that define your character. It gives you strength and perseverance. The life lessons come from loss and from loneliness and despair. Those are the situations that help prepare you for the life you're going to have. When everything is joyous and free, the lessons don't come from that place. They come from the other place.

The students were spellbound.

"Maaannnnn!" said one of the basketball players. "We like you. When are you coming back again?"

*   *   *

Janice Cooley and Herd running back Art Harris started dating in September '70. Around the start of November, she noticed a drastic change in her boyfriend's demeanor. "Artie," as he was known by everybody, was always upbeat and animated.

Two weeks prior to the crash, Artie's cool and confident persona quickly morphed into melancholy. His conversations focused quite a bit on death, and he never explained why. "That's all he would talk about," Janice said. "He kept asking me over and over and over again, 'What would you do if I were to die?'"

Death was not a subject that dominated Janice's thinking. After all, she was an eighteen-year-old freshman in her first semester of college. But most importantly, she wanted to be sensitive and comforting, so she never shared her personal feelings about death with Artie. "I really cared for him," she said. "Whenever he asked me that question, I'd tell him, 'Artie, if you died, I'd want to die too.'"

On another occasion, the subject of death came up again when the couple went out for a car ride in Artie's white 1966 Pontiac Bonneville. "One evening Artie and I were driving around outside of Huntington and he noticed three crosses at the top of a hill near the highway," Janice recalled. "Seeing this spurred a conversation about death and the question of what it would be like when you die. There were several other football players in the car with us who joined in the conversation."

A week before the crash, Artie insisted that Janice go to church with him. They went to a Sunday morning worship service at First Baptist, the church that most of Marshall's black students attended. Janice was caught off guard by Artie's request. He was not a frequent churchgoer.

In the coming days, Janice was due for even more surprises from her beau. On the Wednesday night before the crash, they sat in Artie's car and talked for awhile before driving to a friend's house off campus. Artie made a long-distance phone call home to Passaic, New Jersey, to talk to his mother. During the call, Artie talked to her about his sweetheart, and then he handed the phone to Janice. This was Artie's way of introducing his girlfriend to his mom. After the call, they drove back to campus and had another lengthy talk.

Artie proceeded to tell Janice about every aspect of his life in New Jersey that he had not talked to her about previously. The topics ran the gamut from him being a single father to the many details about his parents and sisters and everybody in his neighborhood, including their dogs.

The last time she saw Artie was the day before the crash. The memories of the time they spent together that day are permanently etched in Janice's mind. The two walked over to the gym where the bus that would take the team to the airport was parked. They engaged in a long embrace and sealed it with a good-bye kiss.

Before boarding the bus, Artie gave Janice these instructions: *"If I don't come back, tell my mom to give my clothes away. And I want you to keep my car."*

That Friday was the final farewell. The following night, Artie was gone. "After all this time, that's the one thing that keeps sticking with me," she said. "It was like *he knew* he was going to die."

The night of November 14, Janice was so overcome by grief that she had to be taken to a nearby hospital. The doctor gave her a shot to help calm her nerves. She fell asleep and was taken to Gullickson Hall, where others who were affected by the tragedy were being consoled and treated. By midnight, Paul and Viola Cooley were on the scene. They left Lewisburg, West Virginia, on a moment's notice and made the three-hour drive to Huntington so they could be with their daughter in her time of need.

The day after the crash, Janice tried desperately to come to grips with what happened. She felt the urge to go to Artie's room at the South Hall dorm. Entering the room, she chatted briefly with Artie's roommate Felix Jordan, who was getting ready to leave just as she came to the door. Felix was still numb. He couldn't shake the images of the debris and wreckage he saw from the night before when he and some other Marshall athletes drove out to the crash site right after the plane had gone down.

Alone and engulfed by the stillness of her surroundings, Janice closed the door and lay down in Artie's bed. Sobbing uncontrollably, she stayed in the room for about two hours. On the way back to her dorm room, she was stunned after learning that Arthur Harris Sr. (Artie's father) was also on the plane. The senior Harris, a baker by trade, left home in New Jersey to go to East Carolina to see his son play. After the game, he accepted Coach Tolley's invitation to fly back with the team on the return trip. Janice met Artie's dad earlier that season when he came to town for one of the Thundering Herd's home games. Janice's thoughts focused on the Harris household. Mia Wagner Harris lost a husband and her only son in that air disaster. All that remained of Artie's immediate family was his mother and two sisters.

Janice discovered that Artie wasn't the only person who had disturbing thoughts about the team's flight to East Carolina. During the afternoon of November 14, Janice made one of her routine calls home to check in with family, What she didn't know at the time was that her grandmother, Gertrude Green, had an uneasy feeling. This feeling got more intense as she and Janice continued their conversation. The grandmother expressed her concerns to Janice's mother right after they finished talking. A few days after the crash, Janice was told about her grandmother's premonition. "My mother later told me that following the call, my grandmother said, 'Something is going to happen—not good,'" Janice said. "She felt this *while she was speaking with me.* Several hours later, the plane crashed. My grandmother always *felt* things."

A little over a week after being introduced to Mrs. Harris over the phone, Janice was in New Jersey attending a joint funeral for Artie and his father. She and Artie's best friend, Walt Garnett, drove the Bonneville back and delivered the car to the family. They returned to West Virginia by train. "When I went to Artie's funeral, all the people he told me about (from the week before) were there," she recalled. "That was his way of preparing me. I'm convinced that he had some type of premonition about death and dying. When Artie introduced me to his mother, I think it made her feel that I was very special to him. When I got there (for the funeral), she embraced me that way. She basically brought me into her home, into her family."

In the years following the crash, Janice made a point to stay in touch with Artie's family. After she graduated and moved to New York in the mid-1970s, she was able to make regular visits because New Jersey was only a short drive from where she lived. She enjoyed her visits and maintaining her connection. Eventually, Janice decided it would be best to stop visiting. Janice realized that her presence was a source of agony that Mrs. Harris would just as soon forget if she could. "Through the years, every time I would visit, she would cry the whole time I was there," Janice said. "Artie was her life. And I felt like me being there was a constant reminder of what had happened. It was always very painful, so I stopped going."

That was in 1980. Not long after that, the Harris women left New Jersey for good and moved to Tampa.

In spite of the personal trauma she suffered, Janice never gave serious thought to going to another school. But getting mentally readjusted to pursuing a college degree was another story entirely. It didn't happen right away. Just being on campus, or being downtown, or at Fairfield Stadium, was hard to handle at times. Janice could never escape the numerous reminders of a relationship that ended tragically. Even now, whenever she attends a Marshall home football game, she scans the sidelines to see which player is wearing jersey No. 22—Artie's number.

For a year or so after the crash, Janice felt "disconnected" from campus life. She confesses that she barely went to class in those days. In the meantime, she started dating again. Every weekend, she visited her boyfriend and his family in nearby Charleston, which is about fifty miles away. Those weekend trips were frequent because she wanted to get away from Marshall and Huntington as much as she possibly could. Eventually she regained her focus and developed the confidence that she could move forward from her recollections of a horrible night in November.

The memories never go away. And in some cases, those recollections surface at the most unlikely times. The most notable example of this happened in 2004 when Janice conducted a job interview as a human resources executive for a communications firm. The middle-aged job candidate sat down in Janice's office and handed her his resume. She looked it over and read that he graduated from the University of Virginia.

"Hmmm, Virginia. You know I'm from West Virginia," Janice said.

"I'm familiar with West Virginia," he answered. "I almost went to school there."

"Where?"

"Marshall University."

"Oh, really? Well, I went to Marshall University."

"Yes, I almost went there. In fact, my best friend in high school went to Marshall and he was killed in that airplane crash."

"Whaaaaaaat! Well tell me, *who* was this best friend?"

"Artie Harris."

Janice was overwhelmed, and for that moment—speechless.

"I'm interviewing this guy for a job, and I had to stop and tell him my story, that I went to Marshall and that I knew Artie," she said. "It was just unbelievable that I was sitting there talking to this guy. He knew all about the family. And he knew *everything* about Artie."

*   *   *

It had only been a month or so before the crash that Debbie (Bailey) Bowen broke up with her boyfriend, Bobby Hill, a Thundering Herd cornerback. Debbie, however, was just as devastated by the loss of Joe Hood, Robert VanHorn, and Freddy Wilson.

Wilson, Hood and VanHorn, three of the 'Bama guys, were proud and protective of Debbie, the first black cheerleader at Marshall. Their relationship was more like that of siblings. "They treated me like I was their baby sister," Debbie said.

VanHorn made it his business to give Debbie a much-needed pep talk when he heard about Debbie's break-up. "I was really down," she recalled. "VanHorn sat me down and assured me that I'd meet the right person one day. The talk we had really helped."

Wilson, one of the few black guys on campus who had his own car, always made sure that Debbie would not have to make the twenty-minute walk to an off-campus apartment she shared with her father. After cheerleading practice was over, Debbie waited at the Twin Towers cafeteria for Freddy to come in from football practice and eat dinner. When Freddy finished dinner, he drove Debbie home.

"Every day, he took it upon himself to do that," she said. "Even when it rained, he was right there. Freddy never fussed or complained, and he never even asked me for gas money."

What Wilson did ask was for Debbie to come to Alabama with him, VanHorn, and Hood for Thanksgiving break. He knew that she'd never traveled to the Deep South before. And he had no way of knowing if she'd be able to come. There was one thing for sure. Wilson would never know if he never asked the question. Here's how that conversation unfolded:

"Why don't you come home with us for Thanksgiving? We'll show you a good time."

"Are you *crazy*?" Debbie answered. "You believe my daddy's going to let me go some place with *three* guys? All the way to Alabama! Hmmm, he might though. If you all come over for dinner and ask him face-to-face, he just might say yes."

Debbie didn't know if she'd get the okay or not. But she felt it was at least worth a try. What she did know was that she couldn't ask for permission at the very last minute and expect a yes to her request.

Max Bailey loved football and was a huge Marshall fan. He followed the team closely and attended nearly every home game. Two weeks before the tragedy, Wilson, VanHorn, and Hood came over for Sunday dinner and convinced him that his daughter would be in good hands. Mr. Bailey gave his consent and Debbie was all set to go.

Debbie got to travel south, but her reasons for going had nothing to do with celebrating a holiday. Instead, she went to mourn the loss of some dear friends. "The trip to Alabama seemed like it took forever," she said. "I slept a lot. I was depressed."

The most endearing memory Debbie had of the 'Bama guys was their unwavering support when she decided to try out for Marshall's cheerleading squad. All the Herd's black players encouraged Debbie in her quest, but the fellas from Tuscaloosa were the most vocal. "Since the school had a good number of blacks playing football, basketball, and other sports, there was no reason why Marshall shouldn't have black cheerleaders too," she said. "I learned later on that they (Wilson, Hood, and VanHorn) made it clear that if there were no black cheerleaders, they would refuse to play."

Debbie believes the players from Alabama had no problem taking a stand, because they grew up in the Deep South during the height of the civil rights movement. "They knew that if they didn't give some type of ultimatum, they might not get what they wanted," she explained. "They were willing to put their scholarships on the line for the principle of the thing. That's one of the reasons why they are so important to me. The older I get, the more I realize how willing they were to take that risk and make a difference."

Debbie said that she and the players never engaged in any deep discussions about her being the school's first black cheerleader. What she does remember is a comical exchange they had after a game.

"It sure was good to see some black legs flying up over there (on the sidelines) for a change," VanHorn said.

Debbie laughed in response.

"That's just great, you guys. Thanks a lot."

"They did comment on the fact that they saw me," Debbie said. "They were proud to have some (black) representation, although they said it in a real silly way."

Making history did not come easily for Debbie. There was staunch opposition. During the spring semester of 1970, a group of black students met with school administrators and demanded that blacks be allowed to cheer.

Initially, they were told that Marshall wasn't ready for black cheerleaders. When black student leaders challenged that assumption, they were told it was a matter of blacks not being qualified. As a way to sidestep the qualification issue, black leaders offered a proposal that the school administrators accepted. Black cheerleading candidates were allowed to spend two months working one-on-one with the Marshall cheerleaders prior to cheerleader tryouts, which were held later that semester. These workouts gave the cheerleader hopefuls a genuine opportunity to hone their skills and improve their chances of making the team.

Being a cheerleader was a novel endeavor for Debbie. She had never cheered before, not in high school, not even in the youth football leagues. She developed her athletic skills in gym classes and intramural track (long jump, high jump) while in high school. At that time, organized sports for girls and women was not nearly as prevalent as it is today. After coming to agreement with the school's top brass about this issue, Howard Henderson, one of the black student leaders, approached Debbie and Toni Brown about trying out. They accepted the challenge and started attending the workouts.

Toni and Debbie soon discovered that there was a lot more to cheerleading than what they saw during football and basketball games. Cheerleaders need to be physically fit, but they also need the agility and suppleness to perform the various gymnastic-type moves that are part of every cheerleading squad's routines.

The eight-week-long training session was physically demanding, even for women in their late teens/early 20s who were healthy and motivated. "Although Toni and I were young, we were kind of out of shape," Debbie said. "We stretched and used muscles we didn't know we had. The cheerleaders told us how to soothe our aches and pains."

Debbie and Toni didn't know what they might encounter when the workout sessions began. To their surprise, they were well received by the school's cheerleaders. "The girls were very nice. They never acted like they *didn't* want to work with us," Debbie remembers. "I never doubted my physical abilities to do the job. Quite honestly, I didn't think we would be accepted into the group. I didn't expect them to teach us anything. I thought they would shun us, but they didn't, and I'll never forget their kindness. They taught us everything they knew to prepare us for tryouts. The practices were always upbeat with a lot of laughing and joking. "

Debbie fully appreciates being part of school history. But she readily confesses that her college cheerleader experiences could have been more enjoyable. The impact of the crash and its aftermath had a lasting effect on her mind-set about Marshall. After graduating in 1973, she never saw the need to visit her alma mater. Nearly thirty years would pass before Debbie would return for homecoming.

"I was sad for a long time," she said. "And every time I would think about it, I would cry—hard. And the tears were not the drip, drip kind either. Most people don't look at cheerleaders as being all that significant. But we *belonged* to our team. I was a cheerleader who had to go on without my team. It was a pretty lonely feeling."

As things turned out, it would take many, many years—thirty-nine to be exact—for Debbie to finally get closure on the tragedy. Her breakthrough came. But it was in a most surprising fashion, and it transpired in the most unlikely of all settings: a Marshall football game.

Here's how Debbie remembers it.

It's Homecoming 2009 and Edwards Stadium was bursting at the seams. A capacity crowd was on hand to watch Marshall play East Carolina University. Just minutes before kickoff, Debbie joined five women at the north end of the stadium for a moment of nostalgia. Talk about a flashback trip down memory lane. All the ladies in this group were varsity cheerleaders for Marshall in 1970. One by one, each cheerleader was introduced. When the introductions were finished, the PA announcer directed everyone's attention to the stadium's jumbo-sized television screen. What the stadium crowd saw was an archived color photograph from the 1970 season of the cheerleaders running down the ramp and onto the field with the MU football team.

The revved-up crowd gave a standing ovation for the ladies, who graciously accepted the thunderous applause. Right after that, Debbie and the rest of the '70 cheerleaders ran onto the playing field with the 2009 version of the Thundering Herd. These moments in which the Marshall cheerleaders were publicly recognized did wonders for Debbie. For the first time in a long time, she could move forward in a way that she hadn't been able to in years past.

"I won't ever forget that day," she said. "All of us had a common bond from our time as cheerleaders. We shared the same experiences. When I saw that picture on the big-screen, it was closure for me after all those years. Finally, there was recognition that there were a lot of people who were left behind (in the aftermath of the plane crash). To me, it was like coming to the end of a chapter in a book. After that, I was okay."

*   *   *

Whenever Reggie Oliver goes home to Tuscaloosa, his itinerary always includes a stop at Cedar Oak Memorial Park. Some of Oliver's relatives are buried there, but there's added significance. Larry Sanders, Joe Hood, Robert VanHorn, and Freddy Wilson are buried there too. "I've made it a habit to always stop by and chat with the fellas," Oliver said. "They get the latest updates from me on what's happening at Marshall. I can always feel their presence. I *know* they watch over me. I walk with the angels every day."

The night of the crash is firmly engrained in Oliver's memory. He had gone to the store but rushed back to campus when he heard the news. At that moment, all he could think about was getting to the airport, so he jumped into a car packed to capacity with MU athletes and they took off. After arriving, they parked near the highway and navigated through some heavy underbrush to an unpaved road that took them to the scene of the tragedy.

The gassy smell of burning jet fuel was unmistakable. Oliver and the others were standing only twenty feet away from where the area had been roped off by emergency rescue workers. Oliver knew that everyone—including four guys from his hometown—had perished. But those four were more than *homeboys* to Oliver; he looked up to them. They were like older brothers. "To stand and watch as I did out at the airport that night was very difficult," he explained. "The smoke (from the crash) was so thick, I could smell it in my clothes."

At one point, Marshall had a virtual Tuscaloosa pipeline comprised strictly of people from Druid High School. Sanders arrived in '68, followed by Hood, VanHorn, Wilson, Florzell Horton, and Coach Kenneth O'Rourke the next year. Oliver, the rookie of the "T'town" contingent, joined the crew as a freshman in '70.

Had Horton stayed in school, he most likely would have played that year. But a nagging injury that never healed properly prompted him to leave school right before the start of preseason practice in August of '70. O'Rourke, a graduate assistant, coached the Herd's freshman team in '69. He left after one season and changed his career path. Today, he's an assistant professor of behavioral studies and educational leadership at Southern University (Louisiana).

At some point during the course of each day, Oliver routinely reflects on the night that changed his life forever. The terror of the tragedy is forever inescapable. Yet, in spite of his personal pain, Oliver has managed to move on while maintaining a perspective that keeps him from being sacked by long-term grief. "Having gone through that whole experience, you learn that it's not something you can practice," he said. "There's nothing anyone can do to prepare for that kind of situation. You just respond as best you can. It was a sad time, a bad time. But I don't dwell on that. The memories I have of the '70 team are good ones."

The memories for the former quarterback are many. But there's one item that serves as an unmistakable reminder. It's rare that anyone will ever see Oliver on any given day when he's not wearing a ring that was originally designed for one of the seven seniors on the '70 team. It's a treasured possession. Since the intended recipients all died in the crash, those rings were not presented until a few years after the crash. Coach Lengyel gave the rings to members of the Young Thundering Herd who came onboard in '71 and stuck it out until the end of their senior seasons. Oliver was given a ring that was originally designed for offensive lineman Tom Brown. Tom's name is inscribed inside the ring.

For Oliver, the ring is tangible evidence that Marshall's success in the mid-1980s and beyond started with the sweat and dedication of the '70 team that perished before it could finish what it started. "I've received rings when Marshall won two national championships," he said. "But that ring from '70 is very special. I wear it almost every day. It's a constant reminder."

When Oliver first came to Marshall, he and his four hometown buddies had a dream that they would help orchestrate a miraculous turnaround at Marshall. It was their declared mission. There's a sentiment among the Herd faithful that those who died in the plane crash are continuously working behind the scenes on Marshall's behalf. It's the Thundering Herd's version of the twelfth man.

The twelfth man is hardly the substance of fiction. Those who were on hand to witness the Marshall miracle against Xavier in '71 can attest to that. Even for the skeptics, there's sufficient evidence to support the existence of the twelfth man. Since the opening of Edwards Stadium in '91, Marshall has taken home-field advantage to a stratospheric level. During that stretch, Marshall has a home winning percentage of .847, which is the best in major-college football, according to Jim Gumm, sports editor of

119

The Kickoff, one of the nation's most trusted sources for college football rankings.

The record shows that at the end of 2010, the Thundering Herd had 122 wins and only twenty-two defeats in the home games it played over the last nineteen seasons at "the Joan." That's saying a mouthful when you look at all the perennial powers ranked below Marshall on this list. At home, the Herd has proven to be better than such high-profile programs as Alabama (second/.827), Oklahoma (fourth/.807), Penn State (sixth/.802), Auburn (seventh/.796), Ohio State (ninth/.778), and Texas (twelfth/.777).

"If you believe and have faith, you believe in the unseen," Oliver declared. "When you look at what's happened with Marshall year by year after the crash, there's no way to explain it other than the existence of the twelfth man. The twelfth man has been present and will be ever present at Marshall University. Teams don't know what they're getting into when they play Marshall. They're not just playing against eleven people on the field. They're playing against a force."

The University of Texas-El Paso knows this all too well. The Miners came to town as the Herd's 2010 homecoming opponent. They had no idea they would be central participants in a game that featured one strange twist after another.

With a little over five minutes left to play in the game, UTEP scored a touchdown to take a 12-7 lead. The Miners opted to go for the two-point conversion, but the move proved to be ill-advised. Marshall defensive back Donald Brown intercepted a pass and ran it back one hundred yards to cut the deficit to 12-9.

Time was running out. About three minutes remained in regulation, but Marshall was not done yet. The home team got the ball back with one last opportunity to pull out a win at the very end. The Herd marched to UTEP's two-yard line but was stopped on third down and settled for kicking a field goal that tied the game at 12.

That's when the game turned weirder on nearly every sequence. MU's field goal kick sailed through the uprights, but the Miners were flagged for roughing the kicker. Texas-El Paso's players claimed the ball was partially deflected so the penalty should be waved off. Miners coach Mike Price challenged the call but to no avail. With first and goal at the one-yard line, Tron Martinez ran it in for a touchdown to put the Herd back on top.

That's just what Price wanted. He figured that by allowing Marshall to score quickly, there would still be adequate time (1 minute, 47 seconds) for UTEP to stage a successful game-winning drive. Price's plan almost worked. The Miners drove to Marshall's thirty-one-yard line. But the Herd eventually settled the issue by forcing a fourth-down incompletion. A highly satisfied homecoming crowd basked in the glow of Marshall's 16-12 victory.

"They're very tough at home," Price said. "You have to be ready for a fight from the time your team comes out of the locker room. The Marshall fans are really into it, and the visiting team takes a lot of razzing. That (2010) game was unusual. I didn't make a call for us to try to block the kick when Marshall went for the field goal. Our guys just tried a little too hard, and we ended up getting a penalty. I thought we got a piece of the ball, but it was tough to see on the replay because of the angle. Our plan was to let them kick it so we could get the ball back and give ourselves a chance to win the game at the end."

*   *   *

Larry "the Ice Man" Isom had a nagging premonition about the football team's road trip to East Carolina. He had a gut feeling that it would not be a good weekend for the Thundering Herd. "I told some of the players," he said, "but they never said anything to me. What would they say anyway? It wasn't like they had a choice. They had a game to play. They had to be there, so it meant they had to go on the plane."

The Thursday night before the crash, Isom's room was transformed into a barbershop. He owned his own clippers but didn't cut anybody's hair on a regular basis. Three football players—Bobby Hill, Scottie Reese, and Dennis Blevins—requested touch-up trims for their Afros, and Isom obliged. Isom's dorm room was a hang-out. The door was usually open and the nine-inch black-and-white television set was usually turned on. Most of the time, you'd hear the latest sounds of the Funkadelic, Temptations, Last Poets, or James Brown blasting on the record player.

Larry Isom and Bobby "Bee-Bop" Hill befriended one another as freshmen in '69. On school breaks, Bobby was a frequent visitor whenever Isom went home to nearby Charleston. During the fall semester of '70, they were next-door neighbors at the South Hall dorm.

"Bobby was down to earth, straight-up, and honest," Isom said. "I'd trust him with anything."

Bee-Bop, whose academic major was business, wore a big Afro and sported a gold cap on one of his teeth. Appearance-wise, he was not physically intimidating at five feet, eleven inches and 165 pounds. In Bobby's case, however, looks were deceiving. He could deliver a hit as well as any 220-pound linebacker and was probably the second-fastest on the team next to Joe Hood. Bee-Bop ran 4.5 seconds in the forty-yard dash but was even more impressive over longer distances.

I remember the day when he turned in a blistering 200 meters in the mid-twenty-one-second range on a gravel surface at an intramural track meet. What was so amazing was that he was nowhere close to being in competitive shape for track at that time. Bobby had a well-developed upper body, which explained how someone with such a slight build could match blows with much bigger players.

The seven-day period between the night of the crash and the day of Bobby's funeral was difficult for Isom. The nights were far worse than the days. He had a hard time reconciling the fact that all those players who regularly stopped by his room would never be coming back.

Those weren't the only thoughts running through Isom's head. He was certain that his dorm room had become a temporary night-time dwelling place for an unseen visitor. On at least two occasions, Isom remembers waking up and being overcome by mixed emotions. He felt that somebody was hovering above his bed. It scared him, but at the same time he never felt like he was in danger. "It's hard to explain," he said. "There was a strong presence in my room. And I know it was Bobby. How do I know? I just know. It was unreal. I ended up sleeping with the lights on for four or five nights in a row."

The weekend trip to Dallas, Texas, for Bobby's funeral has always been a blur for Isom. He doesn't recall any specifics about the service, only that it was very sad and very depressing. "What I remember more than anything was that I sat on the front row," he said. "It was just like I was family. Bobby's people treated me that way."

Isom was grateful for the opportunity to travel to Texas for the funeral. Yet the aftermath of the tragedy caused unexpected problems. Staying focused on the books was not easy. Academically, the semester of the crash and that following spring semester were not good ones for Isom. During those semesters, he was virtually missing in action. Isom's grade-point average plummeted to below 1.0. Fortunately, he was able to regroup during summer school and he got back on track to graduate the following year with a bachelor's degree in accounting.

"(At first) I wanted to leave and get away," he said. "I didn't want to be in school anymore. Since my parents were paying my way, I knew that I wouldn't be leaving. And besides, I really didn't want to go anywhere else."

Isom looks back on his college days as a learning experience that has helped him to develop a full appreciation for life and health. In his mind, those who are still alive and well have much to be thankful for. "We are so fortunate," he said. "We have life and health, so we shouldn't complain so much. For those of us who were at Marshall all those years ago, we will always remember. There were so many who lost their lives at a very tender age. To be honest about it, we really are lucky to still be here."

Chapter Nine

Media Treatment of the Tragedy

"I can't even watch it (the movie We Are Marshall). *I've never seen it. Every time it comes on (television), I start crying."*

Al Evans
Marshall graduate
Class of 1973

The resurrection of Marshall University football is one of the most amazing episodes in all of sports. First, there's the terrifying plane crash that comes so close to wiping out an entire team. Second, the school refuses to abandon the sport and takes on the grim task of rebuilding. The restoration process is agonizingly slow, but eventually the Thundering Herd ascends from dire straits to stardom. All those elements come together to produce a story that's uplifting and inspirational.

It took thirty years for this story to finally get the national notoriety that was long overdue. The drought was broken in the year 2000 when the first documentaries about the crash and its aftermath were released *(Ashes to Glory* and *Remembering Marshall)*. After that, another documentary was produced *(Return of the Thundering Herd)*, along with a book *(The Marshall Story)* and a feature film *(We Are Marshall)*. Why did it take so long? Consider the following observations:

- There was never a question about the story's ability to attract an audience. The school had been approached about media portrayals of the tragedy and aftermath. The chief concern for school officials was giving their okay for a production that would treat the subject matter with sensitivity while honoring the memory of those who perished. For a long time, no agreements to produce a documentary or movie were ever finalized.

- For the families, friends, and loved ones of those who died in the crash, the pain was deep and lasting. In several cases, people who had much to contribute to a movie production found it too painful to relive their recollections. They declined to participate. Many years would pass before those who were close to the '70 tragedy would feel compelled to share their memories and insights.

- It took three decades for this story to run its course. Marshall U. football didn't reach its zenith until the tail end of the '90s. The Herd finished the '99 season as one of major-college football's elites at No. 10 in the national rankings of The Associated Press and the Coaches final polls.

Ashes to Glory (John Witek and Deborah Novak) and *Remembering Marshall* (ESPN Classic) served as the breakthrough media projects for the Marshall story. Both documentaries used the same approach in artfully incorporating people who were on hand at the time of the tragedy. Interviews with players and coaches who didn't make the ill-fated trip, plus memories of friends and loved ones of the crash victims, portray a real-life, first-hand description of what actually happened on that night. These personal accounts also help viewers to better understand the process MU went through in picking up the pieces. The release date of these documentaries coincided with the thirtieth anniversary of the crash.

Return of the Thundering Herd came out several weeks before the premiere of the feature film. Produced by Warner Bros., this documentary was billed as the story that inspired *We Are Marshall*. Hollywood used this documentary DVD as a marketing tool to create heightened interest in the movie in the weeks leading up to its nationwide premiere during Christmas week of 2006.

Return of the Thundering Herd wasn't the only tie-in to the movie. *The Marshall Story* provides a year-by-year chronology of the football program. The starting point goes back to the time period before the '69 recruiting scandal and runs all the way through the decade of the '90s (era of Herd nirvana) to the mid-2000s. Authored by a team of journalists who covered

MU football for over three decades, the book delivers a detailed account of what happened with the program and why.

We Are Marshall focused mostly on revealing the emotions and frustrations of a school attempting to regroup as portrayed through the characters of two coaches (Jack Lengyel and Red Dawson) and two players (Nate Ruffin and Reggie Oliver). The crescendo moment of the film was Marshall's game-winning score on the final play against Xavier University.

The movie had a huge advantage over other media presentations in getting the story out about Marshall to a widespread audience. Warner Bros. had the budget, distribution, and marketing mechanisms to put Marshall on a national stage. The film had gross receipts of nearly $33 million in its first twenty days on the screen. That figure does not include the income generated from the movie being shown on Home Box Office, Cinemax, Turner Broadcasting, and Showtime, nor does it include DVD sales and the pay-per-view showings offered by cable television companies around the country.

The making of a movie typically creates a lot of buzz, and *We Are Marshall* was no exception. For those who were at MU back in the day, it was difficult not to look back in retrospect. There were many times when memories I hadn't consciously thought about in years would surface. Not only that, but the buzz and anticipation combined to create a reunion kind of atmosphere. From the spring of '06 until early '07, there was chatter everywhere: on the phone lines, via e-mail, and on the World Wide Web.

I never thought about taking on a book-writing project. And up until now, I was always surprised when asked when I might make the transition to being a book author. My interest had always been directed at writing for newspapers and magazines. Coming up with a worthy topic was the chief reason why I opted to stay in my journalistic comfort zone. The thought of me writing a book crystallized only a few years ago. But the process of coming to that conclusion—unknown to me at the time—started in the year 2000. What follows is a description of the chain of events that convinced me that my personal story, coupled with the memories of former schoolmates, was a story that needs to be told.

I was never included in any documentary, movie, or news article about Marshall's football past, yet there was still a personal connection in a roundabout kind of way. The year 2000 marked the thirtieth anniversary of the plane crash. That same year, ESPN Classic produced a documentary titled *Remembering Marshall*. I got involved initially when Ed Carter recommended me as an interview source for the project. When ESPN called, I repeatedly emphasized that I did not play football in '70. That was very important to me. I didn't want to give the impression that I was part of the team for that year when in fact I was not.

When ESPN called in the spring of 2000, I was a sports writer at the *News & Record* daily newspaper in Greensboro, North Carolina. College sports and arena football were my primary beats. The ESPN contact (a woman whose name I don't remember) was interested in featuring me in a segment for this documentary. The plan was for the production crew to come to North Carolina on a weekend when I covered a home game for Greensboro's arena league team.

I was never totally comfortable with the idea, mainly because I thought they'd be far more interested in somebody who was actually on the team that year. And besides, they were the ones who approached me, not the other way around. It's not like I was pleading for publicity.

The phone discussion lasted thirty, maybe forty minutes. And I have to admit that I enjoyed sharing my insights. This was a subject that I rarely—if ever—talked about. Even to this day, the people I worked with in Greensboro probably didn't know that I played ball at Marshall and have a personal connection to the crash and its aftermath. If they did know, they didn't get the information from me. It still amazes me that the folks at ESPN expressed so much interest in getting my input.

The proposed ESPN segment with me in it never materialized. After that first phone conversation, I never heard from them again. I learned later that a film crew attended a church service where Ed Carter preached and he was interviewed afterward. Ed's interview, however, didn't make it past the final edit. Like me, he's nowhere to be seen in the *Remembering Marshall* DVD.

My guess is that the producers changed their minds and opted to focus on other aspects of the story. It would've been interesting to see how my proposed segment would have turned out. There are so many avenues to pursue with the plane crash story. There were so many people left behind who were impacted in one way or another. And in every case, every perspective has value in painting an accurate picture of the raw emotions produced by the tragedy.

My perception of my ties with Thundering Herd football changed completely after watching *Ashes to Glory* for the first time. This Emmy Award-winning documentary had been out for nearly a year before I knew of its existence. I returned to Marshall for the first night of homecoming weekend in 2001, my first homecoming visit in almost twenty years. I was in town for maybe ninety minutes when Vic Simpson, a college classmate, handed me a videotape. I glanced at the title on the cassette written with a black felt-tip marker. Vic wouldn't elaborate on the tape's contents. Guess he wanted me to see for myself.

"I taped this the other night. You're gonna wanna see this."

"What is it?"

"Herd football in 1970, and you're in it."

"Naaaaaaah. That couldn't be. *You know* I didn't play ball that year."

"Yeah, I know. Like I said, you're gonna wanna see this."

There was no time for me to look at the tape that weekend. I was on the run—literally. Because of my job responsibilities as a sports writer for a daily newspaper, I stayed for just one night. I was due back in North Carolina the next night to cover a football game. All during the weekend, I wondered, *What is on that tape that's of so much interest to me personally?* I was surprised and puzzled. Other than being a former teammate, I had no direct link with the '70 Herd. There was no viable reason for me to even be mentioned with that team.

I didn't know it, but I was in for a mild shock. There's a segment in the documentary in which some of the key defensive players from the '70 season are talked about. One of the first players mentioned is safetyman Felix Jordan. But the pictures that were supposed to be of Felix were actually pictures of me from the previous season. Felix and I played the same position and he was given my jersey number (21) after I left the team. But even more amazing was that in several subsequent references to Felix, there were still other photos of me that were used.

There's one sequence that I'll always view as an ominous reminder about my football-playing days at Marshall.

It could have been me on that plane in 1970.

The sequence from *Ashes to Glory*:

Rick Meckstroth, a '70 freshman, recalls his conversations with several players as they prepare to board the bus going to the airport on the day before the crash. Meckstroth finishes talking and the voice-over commentator speaks: "*Felix Jordan, who had an ankle injury, was pulled off the traveling squad at the last minute.*"

Right at the moment Felix's name is mentioned, a picture of *me* splashes full-frame across the screen. There's something that's not right about this picture. It's the wrong No. 21. Felix was spared because of a spur-of-the-moment coaching decision. Still, I couldn't shake this thought: *What would have happened had I opted to play another season?* If that had happened, there's no doubt that other than being injured, I would more than likely have been on that flight.

Whenever I watch the documentary, that one segment always serves as a not-so-subtle reminder. The choice I made the year before the crash was truly a life-saver.

The case of mistaken identity with me and Felix, I'm told, did not go unnoticed when the documentary had its premiere showing in Huntington in November 2000. The producers were made aware of the error immediately, and they got it right when the original documentary on videocassette was made into a DVD.

There are no prominent shots of me in the DVD version of *Ashes to Glory*. All images of me on the VHS tape were removed and replaced with photos of Felix, which is the way it should have been all along. Still, it amazes me how the wrong visuals of Felix managed to make it through editing the first time.

There is a reasonable explanation. *Ashes to Glory* did not have a huge operating budget. As a result, filmmakers Deborah Novak and John Witek engaged in the tedious process of poring through hundreds of archived newspaper photographs and choosing a select few for the documentary. Novak told me during a phone conversation that none of the pictures had names on them and they were assured by those familiar with the '70 team that they had the right names with the right faces.

It's an odd thing about the photographs and proof sheets featured in *Ashes to Glory*. I had seen those before—even the pictures that had incorrectly ID'ed me as being Felix Jordan. When I worked part-time in the *Herald-Dispatch* sports department in the early '70s, I remember curiously sorting through this folder of Marshall football pictures. Most were taken on media day from the 1969 and 1970 seasons. My memories are so vivid that I can visualize the crop marks on the pictures as well as the circles made in grease pencil on some of the proof sheets.

It took a long time before Bill Dodson could reflect on the tragedy in a constructive way. Watching *Ashes to Glory* changed his thinking about his time at Marshall. "I did not have any sense of closure," he said. "I think the pain was repressed like a form of post-traumatic stress which may have affected others differently. After the viewing the film (in 2000), I had more perspective on the crash and felt compelled to reconnect with Marshall." Bill Dodson authored an initiative in Nate Ruffin's name as a means to spur increased black alumni support for the school's $100-million fund-raising campaign.

We Are Marshall is supposed to be a true story. At least that's what viewers are led to believe. At the start of the movie the words "This is a true story" appear prominently in large letters at the top of the screen. That's simply not the case. What's portrayed in the film is more fiction than fact.

For those who lived through the ordeal of November 14, the movie stirred up haunting memories of a horrendous time. Folks around Marshall and Huntington were happy that the story was given a national platform through cinema. For many, the emotions associated with the heavy grief from many years ago still remains. Albert Evans, a sophomore in '70, remembers all too well, and he gets choked up every time. "I can't even watch it," said Evans, a 1973 Marshall graduate. "I've never seen it. Every time it comes on (television), I start crying."

Although Ed Carter is a central figure in the real-life Marshall saga, his character is not portrayed in the movie, and it's by his own choice. After reading the script, Ed declined to sign a release that would have allowed Warner Bros. to use his name and likeness. "I didn't believe it was in the Lord's will for me to be in a production with profanity," he said. "So I was never in it."

It's been a few years since *We Are Marshall* first came out, and Ed has yet to see it. But thanks to those people who have seen the movie and who also know Ed, he's very familiar with what takes place in the flick from one scene to the next. Even though Ed isn't mentioned in the script by name, one of the movie's "composite" characters bears a strong resemblance to how Ed looked during his playing days. This black muscular lineman sports an Afro hairstyle like Ed and also wears Ed's jersey number (77).

"Profanity was my initial reason for not agreeing to participate in the movie," Ed said. "I might watch it at some point. But for now, I just haven't made the choice to watch it."

Ed isn't the only missing ingredient in this production. You won't see Felix Jordan's character in *We Are Marshall* either. Warner Bros. made multiple attempts to contact Jordan but was unsuccessful, which left it with no alternative but to proceed without his input.

Jordan acknowledged receiving a letter from the filmmakers. He made several phone calls but never got a response. According to Jordan, it wouldn't have mattered if he had talked to Warner Bros. because he had already decided that he would not sign his rights away to be in the movie.

In the days leading up to the movie's premiere, Ed gave me Felix's phone number and I called him. I hadn't seen or talked to "X-Ray" in over thirty years. *We Are Marshall* got reams of publicity prior to its initial showing and there was much anticipation among anyone with any kind of connection to Marshall University. Felix, however, was apprehensive about watching it. After mulling it over, he went to see the movie with a group of former Xavier players who competed against Felix in the 1971 game.

"I was thinking about not going because I wasn't sure how I might react," Felix said. "It wasn't as bad as I thought it would be."

The film scores big in recreating the depth of bereavement felt by the Marshall campus and the community. And it's a relief to see that the producers took great pains to ensure that this movie is more about overcoming adversity than winning football games.

Still, there are some issues that bother me.

- Paul Griffen, Annie Cantrell, and Tom Bogdan (Nate Ruffin's roommate) are prime characters. Griffin had a son who died in the crash; Cantrell was the fiancée of Griffin's son; Tom overslept and missed the bus to the airport, so he didn't make the trip. He was so distraught over the tragedy that he never played the game again. Each one appears to be a good fit for the storyline except for one noticeable detail. All three are purely fictional. They never existed in real life.

- Aside from Coach Tolley, you don't get to know anything about anyone else on the '70 team. The audience never learns that Ted Shoebridge, the Herd's starting quarterback, was recruited by every major college in the country. You are never told about the four players from Alabama who were the first in their families to attend college.

- The scene where the coach gets this brilliant idea to switch Reggie Oliver from wide receiver to quarterback is bogus. Oliver played quarterback in high school, was recruited as such, and was the freshman team's QB. Yes, he played wide receiver in the spring of '71, but it was only temporary and he moved back to his original position. I admit that I'm sensitive about this, and I'm not apologizing. In the early '70s, black quarterbacks at white schools were as rare as polar bears in Panama. Oliver was one of a handful of black QBs at mainstream schools who played in an era that preceded Warren Moon (University of Washington) and Randall Cunningham (University of Nevada-Las Vegas). During the decade of the '70s, Oliver, the starting quarterback for the Jacksonville Sharks of the World Football League ('74), was the only former Marshall star to make it to the pros.

• In the movie's final scene, the game-winning play is mostly fantasy. The Herd did win on a last-play-of-the-game pass, but how it all transpired in real life was quite different. The audience is told that the play is a screen pass. But what the audience sees is Oliver scrambling and throwing to Terry Gardner, who makes a fingertip catch in the end zone. That's not a screen pass. And that's not the way it really happened. And besides, as good a runner as Gardner was, catching passes was not one of his strengths. The particulars involved in the real-life ending were far better than what the producers conjured up for the film's defining moment of triumph.

The movie would have been more true-to-life if the producers had run the original play. By using tools, such as slow motion, freeze frames, close-ups, and varied camera angles, the filmmakers could have done a more effective job of accurately reproducing the anxiety, anticipation, and emotional highs of that moment. The screen pass in real life was executed so perfectly that when Gardner caught it, he had a blocker in front of him with only one defensive player to beat. Terry would've scored even if it was touch football.

In terms of context, that's important. That game-winning touchdown represented one of the few times that Marshall did everything right in a season where things didn't go its way very often.

After reading a few news articles and reviews, I'm still baffled as to why people think it's okay for a so-called "true movie" to embellish the facts. The rationale is that as long as the true spirit of the movie's plot comes through, all is well. The movie should've been advertised as "based on a true story." That would have been a more accurate portrayal. *We Are Marshall* deserves kudos for effectively tugging at people's hearts. That's all well and good if you're clueless about the truth. The Marshall story is full of ironies and curious coincidences. It's also a case study of tragedy and triumph. It's a wonderful story and needs no doctoring. It would've been a nice touch on Warner Bros.' part to pursue the movie in the spirit of revealing *all* of the truth and allowing the story to tell itself.

It matters to me that the script failed to deliver the real-deal account of the story. I'm not the only one who feels that way. There are still enough of us around who know what actually happened. Admittedly, there were scenes in the movie that when I first saw them, I couldn't say those things didn't happen because I wasn't sure about some of the details. But after collaborating with former schoolmates by phone and e-mail, I learned that my initial reaction about the movie's accuracy was on point.

"The movie was wrong from the start," said Dickie Carter. "The scene where the players get on the plane laughing and joking around after losing a game would have never happened under Coach Tolley."

Chuck Landon, a fellow Marshall graduate who is now a veteran sports columnist in West Virginia, agrees with Dickie. Chuck wrote some unpopular commentaries about the film during its production and after its release. In Chuck's view, *We Are Marshall* didn't do justice to the memory of the crash victims. Even before the movie came out, he was leery about the filmmaker's willingness to steer clear of fictionalizing a factual story.

Example: One of the movie's basic premises involves assistant coach Red Dawson, who was not on the plane because of a recruiting trip. According to the movie, Dawson was so emotionally distraught about the crash that he emphatically turned down an offer to take over as Rick Tolley's successor. In real life over forty years ago, the exact opposite happened. Dawson wanted the job but was never on the school's shopping list for a new football coach. He never even got an interview. The film's consistent disregard for the truth is a source of irritation for Landon.

"I watched it once and only once," he said. "They (Warner Bros.) didn't care what the facts were. They did whatever they pleased. Before the movie came out, I was hoping they wouldn't mess it up too bad. Then afterward, I was so disgusted. In the *worst possible way*, they exceeded my expectations. The story is good enough on its own to tell it straight-up. It's important because it's about the people that we're remembering who lost their lives. *The least* we can do is to remember them accurately. Give them that respect."

Craig T. Greenlee

We Are Marshall may have saved face to some degree when Terry Gardner signed his release. The release allowed Warner Bros. to use his name and likeness in the movie. Illness prevented Gardner from submitting his release until right before the end of production. Gardner, by the way, never got to see the movie. He died in August 2006, four months before the film's premiere.

According to Landon, movie insiders told him about an alternate plan they would implement. If Gardner hadn't given his written consent, the filmmakers would've employed a white actor to play Gardner, who was black. This new character would go by the name of Billy Bob, and he would be the one to score the winning touchdown in the upset of Xavier. Thank goodness that there was no need to put that alternate plan into action. Had that happened, it would've been another travesty of the truth.

There's another valid reason why Chuck felt shaky about Warner Bros.' treatment of the tragedy. Playing fast and loose with the facts is nothing new for filmmakers. Hollywood has a history of tinkering with subject matter to the point of distorting truth. One of the most glaring examples: *The Express.* This 2008 flick is about All-America running back Ernie Davis who played at Syracuse University in the late '50s/early '60s. Davis, the first black athlete to win the Heisman Trophy, was considered a can't-miss prospect with the Cleveland Browns. The Syracuse star would have teamed up in a dream backfield with the legendary Jim Brown. Davis's pro career never started. He died of leukemia at age twenty-three before he could ever play one down in the NFL.

Davis's former teammates were not enamored by what they saw when they attended the premiere of *The Express.* They gave the movie a resounding thumbs-down rating because of numerous factual errors. At the urging of former teammates, Ger Schwedes, who captained Syracuse's 1959 national championship team, was prompted to write a letter to the *Post-Standard* newspaper in Syracuse, expressing his dismay and disappointment at how the story was presented on film. Schwedes wrote:

> As a work of fiction, the movie is terrific. But that's not the way it was. Because so many of the '59 members have called, e-mailed and written to me with their objections, I'm compelled to set the record straight.

My interest in telling my version of the Marshall story was piqued to an even greater degree after reading an article in a North Carolina newspaper

134

that was published around the time of the *We Are Marshall* premiere. The story focused on Wake Forest University's football coach Jim Grobe, whose hometown is Huntington, West Virginia. He was a college student at the time of the tragedy, but did not attend Marshall. Grobe found out about the crash on his return from an away game during his freshman year at Ferrum Junior College (Virginia). Rick Tolley was an assistant at Ferrum prior to coming to Marshall.

For Grobe's wife Holly, the memories are still painful. Mrs. Grobe grew up in Huntington, and her best friend, Kathy Heath, lost both parents in the crash. Emmett and Elaine Heath were ardent supporters of Marshall athletics.

Coach Grobe is acutely aware of what happened, but there's no way he could have the same perspective of a former player who was at Marshall at that time. The more I thought about it, the more I realized that I had sold myself short as a viable source of information about the Marshall plane crash.

An unexpected encounter I had with a man that I had never met provided further confirmation about getting my story published. One day I was browsing the DVD racks at Wal-Mart. Usually, I don't browse for more than ten minutes. But this time, I spotted a couple of videos about Marshall that I had never seen. I wanted to know more, so I took the time to read all the information on each DVD case. As I read the promotional copy for *Return of the Thundering Herd,* this middle-aged white gentleman, who could see what I was reading, walked up to me. Without introducing himself, he immediately started to discuss the crash. I was blown away. What could have prompted him to do what he did? It's not like I was wearing a Thundering Herd cap, or sweatshirt, or lapel button.

He spoke in great detail about the time he flew into Tri-State Airport just one week after the Marshall plane went down. He described the landscape and the visible evidence of where the plane rammed itself into the side of the mountain, which created a large swath of scorched acreage, much like what you might see in the days following a forest fire that had been put out.

As this stranger continued to speak, I nodded and said nothing. It was all I could do to keep my jaw from dropping to my knees. His description of the area was so precise. All during this one-way conversation, I never told him about my connection to Marshall. The more he talked, the more I was reminded of what the terrain looked like as seen from the passenger window of an airplane coming in for a landing at that airport. Almost instantly, I envisioned the sights from my first time flying into Huntington when I left home at eighteen for my freshman year of college.

This was so eerie.

After reading the story on Coach Grobe, I was moved to make a few phone calls. At first, I got in touch with one of the local television stations and had planned on doing an interview. But after considering how TV tends to be more about sound bites and not much about in-depth insights, I reasoned that a newspaper interview would be a lot better. So I zipped an e-mail message to Terry Oberle, who was the *Winston-Salem Journal*'s sports editor at that time. After giving him a brief synopsis about my time at Marshall, *I just knew* he would assign somebody to interview me. Terry wanted to know more, so we met one afternoon and I shared some of my recollections with him.

What happened next came as a total surprise. Instead of being interviewed, Terry asked me to write the story from a first-person perspective. No limits on story length. In the back of my mind, I was never confident that any newspaper would make adequate room in its sports section to run such a lengthy story in its entirety. Based on my experience as a copy editor and layout and design artist at a daily newspaper, I understood the rationale used to determine which stories run and how prominently those stories are positioned in the paper. The *Journal*'s sports section places heavy emphasis on Wake Forest University and the Atlantic Coast Conference; the major pro sports; Winston-Salem State University; stock car racing, and local minor-league teams.

Those are the paper's high-interest items. That's what their readers want to read about. However, that also meant that any realistic chance of my lengthy story running in the *Journal* was really a long shot. In spite of my reservations, I decided to exercise some patience and wait for the time when the story might run. After completing the story at the start of 2007, one of the paper's photographers took some studio shots of me to run with the article, which would also include some old college photos that I provided.

January, February, March, April . . .
The story had not run yet. Not all that surprising.

May, June, July, August, September . . .
Still no go.
October, November, December, January . . .
A full calendar year had gone by.
Status of the story?
Still on the shelf.

So I called the newspaper and yanked the plug. I didn't have to ask Terry why the story was never published. I already knew. For the reasons that were addressed earlier, it was clear to me that my lengthy story would never get the space it needed. Available editorial space for sports sections in daily newspapers all across the country is shrinking. Not only that, but those items of core-readership interest will always take top priority, which is the way it should be.

I thanked Terry for the opportunity and explained that I had decided to go in another direction. What the story needed most was a different venue. It needed a platform that would grant me the freedom to tell the story in every facet with no restrictions on length and no concerns about whether it would ever be published. From that point on, *November Ever After* developed a life of its own.

Chapter Ten

It's Always with You

Given that Marshall's family of black students was fairly close-knit, it's baffling as to why we never engaged in any meaningful discussions about the tragedy. Yes, we were a community, but that doesn't mean that all of us were bosom buddies.

The plane crash was traumatic, gripping, and surreal. The personal pain and anguish ran so deep. Everybody felt it. In terms of our willingness to discuss our experiences, we were like soldiers who come home after being in combat. Soldiers seldom talk about what happens in a war zone. Typically they say very little, if anything at all. For whatever reason, black students maintained a collective silence about November 14, 1970. Why was that? I have no idea. Maybe it was a matter of us not knowing how to express what we had consciously or subconsciously internalized. Perhaps we unwittingly took the path of least resistance as our chosen means to cope with significant loss. We were content—and very comfortable—at keeping our thoughts, emotions, and viewpoints to ourselves.

"It's hard to explain emotions," said fellow student Bill Redd. "It (plane crash) created a big void that everybody felt immediately. We were in denial, and it hurt so badly. We didn't know what to do. We were introverted and it just continued to fester on our insides. We would've been better off by letting it all out. We needed to talk about it. We needed to find a way to work through it."

For what seemed like eons, Janice Cooley had no desire to share her recollections of the crash and her efforts to recover from the suffering she went through. Losing her boyfriend (running back Art Harris) was horrible enough. She realized that Artie wasn't the only casualty. She was also keenly aware that there were so many others who suffered untold agony. Even now, Janice comes to tears when talking about the tragedy and the days, months, and years that followed.

"Although it's been more than forty years, it's still a sensitive subject for me," she said. "I always looked at it (my personal feelings) as something that's very private. When I was first approached (about doing an interview for this book), I was reluctant. Then I thought, *This is something I need to do.*"

The degree to which we didn't talk among ourselves became very evident as I contacted former schoolmates to tap into their insights and memories about their time at Marshall. True, we were all part of what happened. But even after all this time, I learned that there's still so much new information that many of us who were left behind know little or nothing about. This happened over and over in every interview. It happened so frequently that I lost count of the times when I responded, "This is the first time I've ever heard that."

This previously unknown info covers a wide body of topics and issues associated with Marshall football from that period of time. In several instances, these revelations go beyond the events from the night of the disaster and delve deeply into the human side of those who were left behind and how they opted to deal with the tragedy long after the plane crash victims were laid to rest.

In retrospect, I suspect that we were products of our college-day era. There were no probing discussions about how we were impacted because there was no model for us to follow. Grief counseling—as we know it today—was nonexistent back then. There was no professional counseling available for us like there was for those involved in the tragedies at Columbine High School in Colorado and Virginia Tech University. I believe that many of us selectively blocked out specifics of events associated with the plane crash. *Blocking out* served as a sedative of sorts to help ease the suffering.

Former cheerleader Debbie (Bailey) Bowen started blocking out in the days immediately following the crash, and the process didn't end until thirty-nine years later when she returned for a homecoming weekend.

At first, Debbie refused to believe the news reports. In her mind, it just had to be *some other* plane that went down. The harsh reality hit home when she was asked to visit the temporary morgue to identify some personal effects that belonged to Joe Hood, one of the players from Tuscaloosa, Alabama.

When Debbie learned that everyone was burned beyond recognition, she made it clear that she was unavailable. "Immediately, I said, 'Absolutely not,'" Debbie explained. "With the bodies in the condition they were in, I asked, 'Why would I want to subject myself to that?' I never wanted to see that (charred bodies). They had a ring that supposedly belonged to Joe and they thought I would probably recognize it. When we got back from the funerals and school started again, I tried to get over it. I walked around in a state of confusion."

More than forty years after the fact, there's a willingness to speak freely and share personal insights about November 14, 1970. Up to now, folks have said little or nothing. Maybe it's because nobody ever asked. Then again, maybe things have changed because so much time has passed that folks no longer want to keep their silence.

I never felt compelled to discuss anything about the crash with anybody, schoolmates included. To my way of thinking, my ties to football had been severed for good, so there was no need for me to talk. Sure, I was a Thundering Herd safety for two years, and I played with most of the guys who died. My decision to quit football was strictly voluntary. There was no career-ending injury. I was never suspended, never kicked off the team.

It would take a few years after the crash before Marshall would experience any sense of normalcy. And yet it's debatable as to when that actually happened. Gina (Starling) Gunn contends that campus life could never return to normal until the freshman class of '70 graduated. "The only time I remember any real conversation taking place about the crash was around time for the anniversary," Gina said. "After that day, it was like it was brushed aside. To me, it seemed like that was everybody's way of dealing with it. There was a new norm on campus, but it didn't occur until after I graduated ('75). Before then, we just went along and dealt with things as best we could."

Once Gina's class graduated, most of the students who had any personal or emotional ties with the '70 team were gone. Those who came after '70 heard first-person accounts from those who were on the scene at that time. But at best, they could only imagine what it was really like. They could never experience the range of emotions from that night, so they could never truly understand the grief and sorrow that weighed heavily on a college campus and a city. Even now, it's still difficult for those of us who were left behind to fully comprehend it all.

Many of us were convinced that our memories of the crash might somehow evaporate once we graduated from school and moved to other parts of the country. This seemed logical. After all, you're not likely to encounter any reminders about November 14, 1970, if you live somewhere else besides Huntington, West Virginia, and its surrounding communities. In reality, things just didn't work that way. Janice Cooley learned this lesson on a West Coast trip a few years back. Just before the start of a business meeting, the subject of Marshall University football came up and the fact that Janice had some close and personal ties to the disaster. One of Janice's colleagues asked her that one personal question that others wouldn't dare ask. Everyone in the group knew it was a touchy topic. But it was okay. Janice knew the question was asked in a sincere and caring manner.

"How do you ever get over something like that?"

Janice paused for a moment. But before she could open her mouth to speak, the colleague supplied the answer that Janice was about to give.

"You don't. You don't."

"She was exactly right," Janice said. "I just wanted to hug her and tell her that."

The semester following the crash was especially difficult. The intensity of bereavement on campus during the spring of '71 wasn't much different from the night the Marshall plane went down. This proved to be a make-or-break time when people made decisions about their college futures. Most opted to remain at MU; others felt they would best be served by a change of scenery. For those who eventually transferred to other schools, the familiar sights around campus and around the city brought back too many sad memories of the players who died. Angela Dodson recalls a conversation she overheard between two coeds on her dorm floor. One of the ladies, a girlfriend of one of the deceased players, bared her soul to a friend about her daily bouts in coping with her loss.

"Are you sure that leaving here is what you really want to do?"

"It's hard for me to go through this every day."

"What's going on?"

"Everywhere I go, I keep looking for him. Every time I turn a corner, I just know that we'll run into each other."

"In time, things could get better, you know."

"If I stay here, I know that what I'm dealing with now will continue to happen. But if I'm on another campus, I won't have to worry about that. That's why I know it's best for me to go."

Songs from that era prompted painful memories too. Aside from "Fire and Rain" by James Taylor, "One Less Bell to Answer" by The 5th Dimension was equally devastating in reminding me about the night when Marshall's plane went down.

A few months after the crash, I was at an off-campus party around two o'clock in the morning. The music was soft and mellow. "One Less Bell to Answer" started playing, and I began to think about those ladies whose boyfriends died on that chilly night in November.

The song deals with the frame of mind of a heartbroken woman. I can't figure out why anybody would play that song at a party, especially a party at Marshall in the days and months following the crash. It's not a record I would play to help set a romantic mood. There's an undeniable link between the song's lyrics and November 14. One verse in particular—"One less man to pick up after"—struck an emotional chord with me. As soon as I heard it, I was weighed down by sadness and could only imagine what Janice Cooley, Macie Lugo, and others who lost boyfriends in the crash were going through.

It didn't help any that the funerals were closed casket affairs. Certainly, it was necessary. In my opinion, that made it even more difficult for us to arrive at some sense of closure. I think it has a lot to do with the morbid sense of curiosity that most folks have but will not acknowledge. People want to see the body of the deceased. A closed casket service interferes with the way people usually come to grips with the loss of friends and loved ones. At most funerals, we're accustomed to seeing the physical remains of the departed.

For crash victims, a framed picture placed on top of the casket was the only visual. I believe that for the most part, people have a desire—and in some instances a need—to touch the deceased and take that final look before burial. With a closed casket funeral, none of that takes place. Therefore, friends and loved ones of the dearly departed are deprived of that opportunity.

Gary Young, a nationally known grief support group leader, is surprised that people affected by the Marshall crash never talked at length about their feelings. He recognizes that grief counseling was not available in '70. For that very reason, he explains, folks didn't talk because they probably didn't know what to say, or how to say it, or were unsure as to whether others would even want to hear what they had to say.

Young is well equipped to deal with the multiple issues associated with grief and loss. He and his wife Kathy coauthored *Loss and Found* (2006), a groundbreaking book about coping with the death of a spouse at a young age. The Youngs' book is written from a layperson's perspective and is considered a must-read for anyone who has experienced loss. *Loss and Found* earned ringing endorsements from a number of organizations, such as Hospice Foundation of America, the city police departments in New York and Los Angeles, Survivors of 9/11, and TAPS (a grief counseling agency for the US military).

Because the crash happened so long ago, it would seem like a waste of energy for folks to discuss their inner feelings after so many years have passed. Young doesn't agree with that line of thinking. In fact, he's convinced that it's the healthy thing to do.

"It's never too late to heal," Young said. "It's never too late to start clearing the atmosphere and putting things on the right path. Once you have experienced a deep grief, you can eventually learn to manage it rather than having it manage you. You're never going to lose it (the memory) because it's so much a part of you. So the idea of discussing it later, no matter how long it's been, is very healing. It's not only healing for the person speaking, but healing for the person listening as well. That's why support groups are so good. It goes both ways."

The Marshall plane crash might be viewed as ancient history for people in the thirty-five-and-under age group. While it's true that many years have passed, it would be misguided to assume that people who went through the bereavement process back in the day ever had complete closure on the matter. Some are satisfied that, for them, closure came over forty years ago when they were part of the Homegoing Caravan.

It took much longer for Debbie (Bailey) Bowen. For me, there's still a process to go through in order to effectively deal with this shocking episode from my past. And I'm confident that there are other former schoolmates who have gone through or are going through the same things.

Taking on this book project has helped in that regard. By talking to fellow alumni, reviewing old news articles and returning to campus for a few days, I was able to remember details from the late '60s/early '70s that I hadn't thought about in years. When I visited the team's memorial at Spring Hill Cemetery in the spring of 2010, it was the first time I had *ever* gone to that cemetery for the sole purpose of seeing the Marshall memorial. In years past, I went to Spring Hill to attend the funerals of kinfolk. If it wasn't for this book, I probably would never have visited the memorial.

The hill where the memorial is located provides a clear view of the Twin Towers dormitory on campus less than three miles away. The football practice fields in those days were located behind the Towers.

At the front of the memorial site are six grave markers with no names, signifying the six players whose remains could not be identified. In examining the blank markers and then looking at the names inscribed on the nine-foot-tall granite cenotaph, I could remember the faces of many of the players who perished. This was definitely déjà vu. I did the same thing the day after the crash when I got a Sunday newspaper and looked at pictures of the players and reminisced about them during the years we played together. For those of us who were around in '70, the players who died will forever be young men in their early twenties who were full of life, full of vigor, and full of promise.

There's nothing quite like being at the memorial site in person. More than anything, what I felt at Spring Hill was an abiding sense of calm and peace. The visit served as a viable means for me to reconnect with an integral part of my college past. For me, the process continues. Yet there's joyful consolation in knowing that the labors of my former teammates from long ago helped to produce a fruitful harvest for football.

There is a unique and lasting bond among Marshall's black students from the late '60s/early '70s. That bond transcends the usual ties that college classmates have. The strong connection comes from what we collectively suffered and endured. We are forever connected by the events that occurred over forty years ago at Marshall University. For most of us, there's a special fondness for Thundering Herd football. Our ties to the school are more like deeply entrenched roots that bind us together.

And when you consider what Marshall has accomplished on the gridiron since 1970—two national championships and a slew of bowl game victories, we can proudly say that we remember when. We were witnesses to those lean years when winning was not so commonplace. Back in the day, winning was an every-now-and-then occurrence.

What we can say is that we endured. And during that process, we wept and we agonized. But we also applauded the resurrection of Marshall's football program. And we continue to celebrate the lives of those who perished. With every passing November, checking the calendar to see what day the fourteenth falls on is an automatic for me. Thoughts of the '70 team are fairly constant at that time of year.

The Marshall students from the late '60s/early '70s are on the brink of attaining senior citizen status. We've established ourselves in our careers, raised our children, and, by now, some of us are having a ball as grandparents. Along the way, we've lost loved ones, which includes parents, siblings, other relatives, and, in some cases, childhood pals and lifelong buddies. Even with all of that, we can never erase the memories from over forty years ago, memories that are forever etched in our psyches. True enough, it was so long ago, but it's still just like it happened yesterday. These vivid memories will not fade to black anytime soon.

It's always with you.

My life could have ended on a November night over forty years ago on a muddy hillside in West Virginia. It's so clear to me now that God had another plan.

Appendix

Memories of Marshall

By John Kiesewetter
Cincinnati Enquirer
December 24, 2006

Printed with permission from *The Enquirer*

Felix Jordan of Blue Ash, who might have been on the fateful plane ride, thinks each day of the friends he lost.

Felix Jordan doesn't need to see the new *We Are Marshall* movie to understand the horror of the Marshall University football team perishing in a 1970 plane crash. "I know I'm going to think about it when I open my eyes up every day," says Jordan, 55, of Blue Ash, one of three Marshall varsity players who didn't make that fateful trip to East Carolina University.

"There's not a day that goes by that I don't think about it," says Jordan, a 1969 Sycamore High School graduate who missed the game as a sophomore because he had a severely sprained ankle and was asked by his coach to give up his seat to a team booster.

"I have dreams about my teammates. I have flashbacks, like they're right there next to me. Sometimes I find myself talking to somebody (who died)," says Jordan in his first interview about the crash since the movie project began nearly two years ago. It opened nationwide Friday.

Jordan was hanging out with friends in a Marshall cafeteria in Huntington, W.Va., when they heard about the crash at nearby Tri-State Airport on Nov. 14, 1970. Jordan, freshman quarterback Reggie Oliver and several athletes immediately drove to the crash scene. "We came over this hill and could just see the side of the mountain burning," says Jordan, now a maintenance employee at the Blue Ash Clarion Hotel & Suites. He returned to the wreckage the next day to help recover teammates' bodies.

In all, 75 people died in the crash, including the head coach and most of his assistants; three Moeller High School graduates on the team—Bob Harris, Jack Repasy and Mark Andrews; trainer Jim Schroer, a McNicholas High School graduate; and boosters.

"It was still smoking the next day when we went out to help. There wasn't much there to identify the bodies. I threw up. I couldn't do it."

But you won't see Jordan in the film.

He and teammate Ed Carter, now a Tennessee minister, did not grant Warner Bros. rights to use their likenesses. So screenwriter Jamie Linden tells the story of rebuilding the football team through defensive back Nate Ruffin (Anthony Mackie)—the third player who stayed behind—plus new coach Jack Lengyel (Matthew McConaughey), assistant coach Red Dawson (Matthew Fox) and Oliver (Arlen Escarpeta).

"Nobody was able to reach him (Jordan)," Linden says in a phone interview from Los Angeles.

Jordan says he received a letter from Warner Bros. and called the Los Angeles numbers as requested, but never spoke to anyone about the film. "If they had reached me, I would have talked to them—but I probably wouldn't have signed my rights away," he says. "My friends are more upset about me not being in the movie than I am."

The film, which Jordan saw at a recent preview, depicts the two other returning players as a chubby African-American with an ankle cast and crutches, and a short white player. "We had to change distinct characteristics," Linden says.

Jordan admits he had reservations about recounting the excruciating details for a Hollywood writer.

Life has not been easy for him. He walks with a limp from falling off a ladder. He has bad knees from playing on Marshall's rock-hard artificial turf field. Although he earned a history degree at Marshall and thought of becoming a teacher, Jordan ended up in Detroit installing phone and cable TV systems. Since returning here about 10 years ago, he has worked mostly in motel maintenance.

Jordan, whose younger brother Paul was a Parade All-American running back at Sycamore in 1972, also admits he had used alcohol and drugs to ease his emotional and physical pain. "When something like this happens now, (grief) counselors come to the school. All we had was a Catholic priest to talk to. And he was the team chaplain, and he was as torn up as we were," Jordan says. "They hadn't even come up with the term 'post traumatic stress.' So you had to John Wayne your way through it. Real mean don't cry, and all that. But I cried like a baby.

"People can't understand what you're going through. I tell them: What if you lost 35-40 members of your immediate family, just like that? That's basically what happened. One day they were all there, and the next they were all gone. I get depressed thinking about it. Why did I live? I still don't know the reason 36 years later."

Although he couldn't play, Jordan was scheduled to fly with the team to Greenville. Hours before departure, assistant coach Frank Loria told Jordan he would stay home because his seat on the chartered DC-9 was needed for a former Marshall boosters president. (That is not depicted in the movie.)

Watching the film, Jordan saw his No. 21 jersey on a player during the re-enactment of the 1971 Marshall-Xavier University game. He says he's not surprised that Ruffin, who died in 2001, gets credit for things Jordan says he did, such as calling defensive signals on the field. The film is "about 40 percent accurate," he says. "That's Hollywood. I know they had to make it entertaining," he says. "It was good (not to focus on me) because I'm just naturally introverted. To me, the real heroes were the 75 people in that plane crash."

Bottom line, he's pleased with the production.

"It made Marshall look good, and it didn't make me as sad as I thought," he says. "But most people will go home after the film and can think of something else—but I carry it with me every day."